RECESSION-PROOF YOUR FINANCES

ALAN DOOLEY is a senior finance writer for CHOICE, Australia's leading consumer advocacy organisation. He has spent most of his career researching and writing about financial services for consumer publications in Australia and Ireland.

RECESSION-PROOF YOUR FINANCES

The CHOICE guide to saving, spending and safeguarding your money

ALAN DOOLEY

choice

This book is dedicated to Sarah and Luke.

A CHOICE book

Published by
University of New South Wales Press Ltd
University of New South Wales
Sydney NSW 2052
AUSTRALIA
www.unswpress.com.au

National Library of Australia
Cataloguing-in-Publication entry
    Author: Dooley, Alan.
    Title: Recession-proof your finances: the choice guide to
        saving, spending and safeguarding your money/Alan
        Dooley.
    ISBN: 978 1 92070 551 0 (pbk.)
    Subjects: Finance, Personal.
                Financial crises.
                Budgets, Personal.
                Thriftiness.
    Dewey Number: 332.024

Text design Di Quick
Cover design Design by Committee
Printer Ligare

This book is printed on paper using fibre supplied from
plantation or sustainably managed forests.

Contents

Note to the reader

Every effort has been made to ensure the information in this book is accurate. However, financial products and the markets that underpin them are constantly changing. You should check for up-to-date details before making any decisions. The appendix at the back of the book recommends some good resources and provides links and contacts.

Before deciding on a strategy or particular investments, consider getting licensed financial advice. In an increasingly complex and volatile world, we all need to tap into as much expertise as we can find. This book provides tips on how to find a good financial planner and avoid the pitfalls. You should always read investments' product disclosure statements and providers' financial services guides.

Information in this book is of a general nature and does not take your particular circumstances into account. It does not provide financial advice. Neither the author nor the publisher may be held responsible for any action or claim resulting from the use of this book or the information it contains.

Acknowledgments

A wide range of individuals and organisations helped with the research for this book, and pulling all the data together wouldn't have been possible without their assistance. Many of the organisations are named in the useful resources section with contact details for readers keen to find out more. They include the Australian Institute of Superannuation Trustees, Association of Superannuation Funds of Australia, Financial Planning Association, the Investment and Financial Services Association and the National Information Centre on Retirement Investments. Canstar Cannex, InfoChoice, Morningstar and SelectingSuper supplied investment performance and other financial data. At CHOICE, Elissa Freeman's support and encouragement was much appreciated.

Introduction

Coping with the downturn

The unprecedented events of the last two years have left world financial markets in turmoil. Most of the world's major economies are in recession and it is having an impact on almost every Australian household. After ten years of unabashed spending and borrowing, when for many the notion of actually saving money all but ceased, consumers are at a crossroads. We know the party's over – and it was a wild ride. But after excessive spending on credit and enjoying the good times, how do we clean up the mess?

This book is about finding ways to reduce your expenditure, rein in your debt, protect what you have and plan for the future. It's not just about being frugal and it certainly won't suggest that you stop doing the things that you enjoy in life. But it might help you to spend less, earn more and protect what you already have along the way.

A lot of people are bored – or confused – by the strange world of financial services, which has been described as a system of trading promises, forecasts and guesses about what's going to happen in the future. But fear not, this book is a jargon-free zone. Well that's not quite true, there's jargon here, but it's explained clearly. Who knows? After reading this book you might find yourself at barbecues talking about 'negative economic growth', 'toxic debt' and 'price/earnings ratios'.

If you have money and you want to recession-proof it, there's a very easy and safe way: put it in a government-guaranteed bank deposit account. And that could be a really good idea if a low-risk investment is what you want. It will protect your capital, and may help you sleep soundly at night while avoiding the vagaries of share and property markets. The problem is that in this environment of low interest rates, your money, after tax, may not even keep pace with inflation. You might also miss out on a recovery in share markets, if that happens. There are plenty of investments with supposed higher returns being touted; this book looks at their pros and cons.

But personal finance isn't just about investing. It's also about setting goals and devising sound strategies, borrowing wisely and at the lowest cost, ensuring you have the right level of insurance, and saving and spending your money to the best effect. Uncertainty abounds, with the economy in turmoil and fears about unemployment rising, but there are lots of things you can do to protect your financial future. That's what this book is all about. The government is trying to limit the impact of the global financial crisis, but on an individual level, there are steps we can all take to reduce the likelihood of a 'personal financial crisis'. After all, people don't plan to fail; rather, they fail to plan.

This book doesn't provide financial advice and when it comes to investing, it won't tell you what you 'should' do – that depends on your individual circumstances. But we hope it will help you to:

- take stock of your present situation and determine the health of your 'personal economy'
- get prepared for a potentially rocky road ahead

- cut spending and use your money cleverly – in this era of 'value seeking' , we give you some great money savings tips that you can use every day to beat the system

- save and invest for short-, medium- and long-term goals

- take advantage of the lowest interest rates in nearly 50 years

- hold on to what you have – protecting your wealth is as important as building it, and if you're working, keeping your job is priority number one

- avoid a personal credit crunch – strategies to make credit cards and home loans work for you

- dodge the rip-offs

- get good quality personal advice if you need it

- be ready for the next time.

1

What just happened?

Why the global financial crisis, toxic debt and the credit crunch changed everything.

Just two years ago, it seemed like the good times would never end. Australia was soaring, with more than fifteen years of economic growth: the stock market was enjoying its fourth straight year of almost 20% returns; property was holding its value after a massive boom; and unemployment was at its lowest level in thirty years.

But the events that originated from the US property market crash in 2007 have shaken the world's financial systems to their core. The US 'sub-prime' crisis led to the 'credit crunch', which evolved to the global financial crisis and eventually world recession. Advanced economies are experiencing their deepest downturns since the Second World War. The Asian Development Bank recently put a figure on the value of global financial losses – US$50 *trillion*. Share markets around the world halved in value, with worse results for financial stocks. Banks worldwide have written off $792 *billion* of bad investments and are being bailed out, propped up and nationalised by governments. When Lehman Brothers collapsed, it was the largest bankruptcy in US history.

The US Government has bailed out giant banks and the world's largest insurance company. The British government has saved a number of the country's biggest banks as well. Even Iceland (yes, the country) is struggling to keep its head above water, with inflation exceeding 20%, its three largest banks going down and interest rates at 18%. Iceland's currency, the Krona, fell by up to 150% against the US dollar.

Australia hasn't avoided what is being called 'The Great Recession' – but nobody is sure how long the downturn will last and how bad the things will get. You might be wondering how this whole mess started – in the housing suburbs of America.

WHERE IT ALL STARTED: THE DODGY LOAN CRISIS

Chaos theory, or at least popular culture's representation of it, sees the flapping of a butterfly's wings in Brazil setting off a chain of events that result in a tornado in Texas. Of course, chaos theory is a lot more complicated than that. But the interconnectivity of world economies and investment markets make the 'butterfly effect' a good metaphor for the global financial crisis. How else could families in suburban US missing their mortgage repayments lead to world recession and the collapse of the financial systems that underpin our economies?

There's a saying in financial services that when America sneezes, the world catches a cold. The economic downturn that the world is now experiencing began in the United States, with the *sub-prime* mortgage crisis. Until about 2006, the US housing market was booming. Mortgage lenders were handing out big property loans to risky borrowers. The loans – or more to the point the borrowers – were called 'sub-prime' because that didn't sound as bad as 'dodgy' or 'risky' or 'likely to default'. That many of these borrowers didn't have well-paying jobs didn't matter; the 'American Dream' mortgage legislation and other legislation including an early 1990s Act that required the biggest mortgage lenders to devote a percentage of their lending to affordable housing made home loans available to low-income households. For many people chasing home ownership, such loans were the only way to break into the market. The repayments seemed affordable, as interest rates were low at the time. Often, the loans started off with low, teaser or honeymoon interest rates, lulling borrowers into a false sense of security.

While this was happening, financial institutions and fund managers were packaging up these sub-prime loans and selling them as investments. The so-called financial innovation that resulted led to the creation of strange investments known as collateralised debt obligation (CDOs). The number of these risky US mortgage funds grew dramatically from about 2004, the year to which the global financial crisis can be traced.

While it now seems perfectly obvious that sub-prime mortgage investments were risky, it wasn't so apparent at the time. Reputable credit ratings agencies considered CDOs, which bundled up both safe and risky mortgages, to be 'investment grade' and awarded them excellent credit ratings. US financial institutions sold these collateralised debt obligations to other financial institutions, and they spread around the world. Many of the world's biggest and best-known investment banks were to invest heavily in these investments, which would be later known as *toxic debts*.

TORNADOS IN TEXAS

The real problems began to emerge when US interest rates started to increase. It meant that sub-prime borrowers who couldn't afford their mortgage repayments began to default. This shouldn't have surprised anyone really – the borrowers were, after all, considered risky by the lenders, brokers and everyone else. There was even a name for them – *Ninjas* – for people with 'No Income, No Jobs or Assets'.

Initially, the defaulting sub-prime mortgages didn't seem like a very big deal, as lenders could sell the repossessed properties for a profit. But in 2007, the US house price bubble burst. This was a major problem as all the financial and economic models that underpinned the system were based on house prices continuing to rise. Loan defaults and repossessions started to happen on a large scale, as American borrowers handed back their house keys. US banks were now no longer able to recoup their money when they sold the properties. A glut of houses for sale hit the market, driving prices down further.

Defaulting sub-prime mortgages became a very serious issue for corporate America. Banks realised that the investments and assets on their balance sheets included dwindling collateralised debt obligations. The term *toxic asset* was coined to describe these defaulting loans and their poisonous effect on the creditworthiness of once-venerable institutions. Banks tried to get rid of the bad investments they'd bought, to no avail. Trust in the banking system unravelled; banks stopped lending to other banks because they feared their exposure to toxic debt. And when financial institutions stop lending money to each other on the wholesale market, economists and bankers say that liquidity dries up; what they mean is that interbank lending – often described as the arteries that carry the lifeblood of the financial system – has stopped functioning.

THE STORM SPREADS

A wave of write-downs by banks (where they admit that they have degraded assets) was to follow. We're talking *hundreds of billions* of dollars. Bear Stearns, Wall Street's fifth largest investment bank, put a freeze on investors withdrawing their money from two of its hedge funds that invested in collateralised debt obligations. It would later be taken over by JPMorgan Chase. There was a run on British bank Northern Rock, as savers rushed to withdraw their money. US banking giant Merrill Lynch wrote off $US16 billion of mortgages and was later taken over by Bank of America. The two biggest US mortgage lenders, called Fannie Mae and Freddie Mac, were nationalised.

But the event that really sent shockwaves around world financial systems was the collapse of investment bank Lehman Brothers in September 2008, the biggest ever US corporate bankruptcy. Since then, we've had more banks taken over, nationalised and bailed out by government rescue packages. The US government has made hundreds of billions of dollars available to buy banks' sub-prime debt, while also injecting capital into ailing banks. Washington Mutual became the biggest ever bank failure (its banking assets were sold to JPMorgan Chase). In the Unites States the venerable Goldman Sachs and Morgan Stanley both changed their status from a merchant bank to a 'bank' so they could get help from the government. Now all the 'great' Wall Street investment banks of the past are gone, having submitted to being licensed and regulated like a commercial bank, or having been taken over by one.

WORLD GRIPPED BY 'THE GREAT RECESSION'

By mid-2009, almost every developed nation is in recession. Share and property markets have plummeted. Unemployment is rising and hundreds of billions of dollars have been lost. Unlike the last major recession, where a group of developing countries, Brazil, Russia, India and China, nicknamed the BRICs continued to grow, this time almost every country is affected, including China and Japan, two of our most important trading partners.

The International Monetary Fund (IMF) reckons the pain will continue. 'World growth is projected to fall to half a percent in 2009, its lowest rate since World War II,' the IMF stated in early 2009. 'The world economy is facing a deep recession. Financial markets remain under stress. Anaemic global growth has reversed the commodity price boom. The high level of uncertainty has prompted households and businesses to postpone expenditures, reducing demand for consumer and capital goods. At the same time, widespread disruptions in credit are constraining household spending and curtailing production and trade.'

There's wide recognition that banks, particularly in the United States, need to be repaired before the world can get back on its economic feet. In March 2009, Dr Adrian Blundell-Wignall, an Australian economist who works for the International Organisation for Economic Cooperation and Development (OECD) in Paris, said that Australian banks benefitted from not having major investment bank businesses. 'But those US and European banks that supported their earnings growth through the securitisation of poor quality assests, the risks in which they were not able to transfer to others may yet face technical solvency issues. It's what we can't see, particularly in un-transparent Europe, that continues to be a real worry to me. Confidence in the system can't be restored until that situation is fixed.'

So far, Australia has fared relatively well when compared with most other countries. In fact, when you consider the problems overseas, our quite modest economic decline of 0.5% in the last three months of 2008 and 0.4% growth in early 2009 doesn't seem so bad when compared with the United States, Europe and Japan. Of the OECD countries only Australia and Canada hadn't entered a technical recession by March 2009. But the International Monetary Fund predicts that in 2009 the Australian economy will contract by 1.4%, compared to a contraction of 2.8% in the US, over 4% in the UK and the European Union, and a 6.2% economic contraction in Japan.

However, some are saying the problems for Australia could get worse, particularly given the extent of our national debt. World recession is lapping on our shores and seven of our ten major trading partners are suffering economic contractions. The next chapter looks at the outlook for what many people still see as 'the lucky country' – and more importantly, what you can do to weather this unprecedented financial storm.

What is a recession?

In Australia and most countries, a technical recession is defined as two consecutive three-month periods (or two quarters) of negative economic growth. Others consider rising unemployment the key measure. However, there's no universally accepted definition. In the United States, for example, a group of esteemed university economists decide on whether the world's largest economy is contracting after assessing trends along several key criteria.

Economic growth is measured in terms of Gross Domestic Product, or GDP, which is the total value of all goods and services produced in an economy. You might wonder how an economy can grow negatively. Well, it can't! What the politicians are trying to avoid saying is that the economy is shrinking or contracting. Those terms might be less palatable than 'growing negatively', though they mean the same thing.

As the global financial crisis started to hit, our federal government did its level best to prevent Australia from entering a technical recession by injecting huge amounts of money into the economy. And while it's helped to stimulate economic activity, the outlook remains uncertain in the face of powerful international economic forces.

2

Still the lucky country?

Many debt-laden households need to knuckle down and plan to get through this recession.

Australia has long been thought of as the 'lucky country', due to our great weather, natural resources and high standard of living. Share investors have been lucky too, with our equity market among the world's best performers over the last 100 years. But with Australia teetering on a recession, is the lucky country's good fortune finally about to run out?

At a March 2009 conference run by the Australian Securities and Investments Commission (ASIC), a presenter asked the audience whether they believed our banks had so far got through the global financial crisis (GFC) in reasonably good shape because of good regulation and prudent business practices, or simply good fortune. The show of hands revealed that a large chunk of the audience, which included industry regulators, financial services people and the media, believed that the Aussie banks had been 'just plain lucky' in avoiding the worst of the GFC.

That Australia would eventually experience a downturn was inevitable. Few other countries have escaped unscathed and as an exporting nation we're highly dependent on our trading partners. Most of the countries to whom we sell the majority of our exports are in recession, and if they don't have the money to pay for the stuff we produce, our economy must suffer. Our mining industry, which has been one of the big drivers of Australia's economic success in the last decade, is heavily reliant on Chinese demand for our natural resources. But at the time of writing, the World Bank is forecasting that growth in China, the world's second largest economy, will plunge in 2009. Meanwhile, Japan, our biggest trading partner, is in a deep and prolonged downturn.

The question is where our economy will go from here, how many jobs will be lost and how long the downturn will last. We're not out of the woods yet and the worst could be still to come. A pessimist – or a realist – might say, *'You ain't seen nothing yet!'* with increasing unemployment, falling company earnings and the possibility of further property and share market declines still possible. The last economic depression lasted eight years, and while many economists are predicting a much quicker recovery from this recession (the IMF predicts a slow global recovery starting in 2010), there's little certainty. As the saying goes – History doesn't repeat itself, but sometimes it rhymes. This chapter looks at how well Australian households are placed to cope and what we can do to survive.

CONSUMER CONFIDENCE SLUMPS

Though Australia has been relatively unscathed so far, the strain of the world recession is beginning to show. Despite actions by the federal government and Reserve Bank of Australia to keep the economy going – cutting interest rates by 4.25 percentage points in seven months and giving away billions in stimulus packages – the Australian people, whose optimistic disposition is famed, are worried about the future.

There has been a dramatic slump in consumer confidence in the last two years. In early 2009, Bill Evans, Westpac's Chief Economist, said that in 35 years of producing the Westpac–Melbourne Institute index of Consumer Sentiment never had such a divergence between the current economic conditions and consumers' expectations about the future been seen: 'This indicates that while consumers recognise improvements in current conditions resulting directly from aggressive policy stimuluses, they are unusually fearful about the future.'

Low consumer confidence certainly isn't unique to Australia – it's worldwide. Robert Shiller, a Yale economist who famously predicted the end of the 'dot com' boom at the beginning of the century, calls this a 'negative bubble in confidence'. Irrational exuberance seems to have been replaced by overwhelming despondency and fear – sentiments, which we all hope are equally irrational.

THE FINANCIAL TIGHTROPE

So how are Australian households placed to survive this downturn? Well, the Reserve Bank reports that the household sector is in a relatively sound position, but there's no doubt that many are walking a financial tightrope. The majority of people will negotiate this perilous situation and get to the other side. But many are not ideally placed to weather the financial storm.

Laden with debt

The first problem is our level of debt. The international magazine *The Economist* was talking about this back in 2003, when it stated: 'the profligacy of American and British households is legendary, but Australians have been even more reckless ... there are now concerns that unsustainable rates of borrowing will sooner or later end in tears.'

Well, the tears eventually came, and now households across the country are saddled with huge mortgages over properties, which in some cases, could be declining in value. Associate Professor Steve Keen of the University of Western Sydney says we're in the biggest debt bubble of all time, with Australia's debt ratio now 2.5 times what it was during the Great Depression of the 1930s. There's certainly been some heavy household borrowing and spending and not just irresponsible lending. The upshot is that some people are finding themselves in severe mortgage stress. In many cases, families had disregarded the traditional rule of thumb – that your housing repayments shouldn't exceed one-third of your after-tax income. But thankfully, we had nothing like the extent of 'low-documentation' loans (where money was lent even if the borrower didn't provide the paperwork to verify their income and other details) and sub-prime problems of the US.

Ratio of household debt to disposable income, 1978–2008

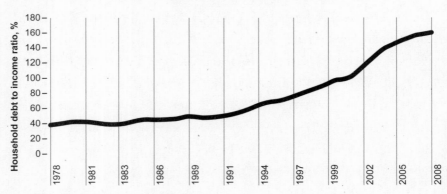

SOURCE Reserve Bank of Australia Statistics

The graph shows the ratio of household debts to our disposable income. In the last ten years the graph took a sharp turn north, as the credit binge took hold. But the problems weren't confined to mortgages – borrowing to invest in shares and credit card and personal loans rose dramatically too. Though the latest available data suggests that credit card spending is starting to cool, the growth in credit card transactions in the previous decade had been enormous. We spent the better part of a decade splurging on credit that enabled us to fund our lifestyles and fill our homes with expensive items. For some people, the notion that you had to actually have money saved up before you could buy things was forgotten. Credit made everything possible – why wait, when you can 'buy now, pay later'?

The good news is that interest rate cuts have dramatically eased the borrowing burden. Chapter 13, 'Avoiding a personal credit crunch' gives strategies to bust those debts and rein in credit card spending. Chapter 14, 'The Mortgage Meltdown' looks at ways for borrowers to take advantage of the lowest interest rates in 40 years – interest rates on mortgages have come down 50%.

DEBT busting

Rainy day savings plummet

Tied to our credit binge was a dramatic change in Australia's savings culture over the last decade. In the mid-1970s households saved, on average, about 15% of their disposable income. By the 1980s the rate had fallen below 10%. A decade later, net household savings had all but disappeared; between 2002 and 2006 the official savings rate was negative. This savings figure doesn't take account of changes in the value of investments in shares and property though, which are reflected in households' overall wealth.

Perhaps the biggest change in consumer behaviour in 2009 and 2010 will be a reversal of our savings rate, which is climbing towards levels not seen since the 1980s. The rate of savings has picked up dramatically in 2009 and is expected to continue to increase as fear about our economic future sets in. It's called precautionary saving.

Chapter 5 gives ideas about how best to squirrel away your money and avoid the traps.

Shares and market-linked investments bomb

After their November 2007 high, Australian shares plummeted by more than 50%, the second biggest fall in the domestic index's history. This has had a dramatic effect on the value of households' financial investments, which include not only shares, but also managed funds, fixed interest investments and superannuation. The graph below shows how the value of financial assets, as a proportion of our after-tax income, rose steeply during the bull market run of 2003 to 2007, but has plummeted since then, as investment markets crashed.

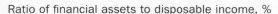

Ratio of financial assets to disposable income, %

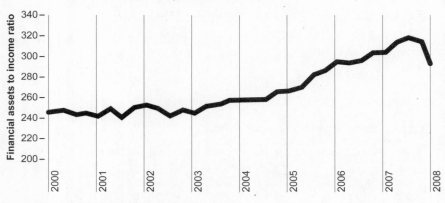

SOURCE Reserve Bank of Australia Statistics

The last two years of share market and property declines have had a dramatic effect on the value of our wealth and retirement savings. This is one of the biggest issues facing investors today, who are asking questions like: 'Will I have enough money to retire?' and 'What options in superannuation are really safe?'

Opinion is divided about where share markets will go from here. In some cases, share prices, as a proportion of companies' earnings, hit historical lows. This could make shares an attractive long-term proposition. And while at the time of writing Australian shares would need to increase about 70% to regain former glories, optimists point out that previous share market recoveries tended to happen quite quickly.

The opposite view is that the present downturn is unlike any share market collapse of the past. This means we can't look to history for any guidance about the future. Company earnings, and not just share prices, have continued to decline.

Chapter 6, 'Investing in shares' looks at ways to invest in shares, and what to consider. We also look at some overseas trends, and whether shares really do always rise in value in the long term. Chapter 9, 'Superannuation – the basics' provides guidance on this complex investment and the following chapter looks at some of the ways you can make sure your fund measures up well.

Never had it so good?

Believe it or not, the Great Recession could make your life more affordable – unless you lose your job. In fact, the 90% or more of people who don't become unemployed will end up managing just fine in this environment. 'The majority of people will be objectively better off, though not emotionally better off,' says ANZ's Chief Economist Saul Eslake. 'Those who keep their jobs will be better off through decreased mortgage repayments, cheaper petrol and cash handouts from the government. But the fear of joining the dole queue, or for older people closer to retirement age, the need to rebuild retirement savings, will mean many people become much more conservative in their spending behaviour even though in many cases they're doing better than before the downturn.'

The property prices bubble

The next big risk is that much of the wealth of households is tied up in bricks, mortar, and land. That doesn't just mean the family home, but investment properties too. Many people bought into the belief that it's important to get on the property ladder – at any price. While there were some warnings over the last five years that property prices were in a bubble, they were often drowned out by messages – often from vested interests in the industry – that property was 'good value' and would continue to appreciate.

The market has cooled and declined – though not like the United Sates or the United Kingdom. But here's a pretty alarming statistic: the median house price in Sydney, our most expensive city, is over eight times the median household income in that city. This is worrying because that income to house price ratio is even higher than that of a country like Ireland *before* its property market crashed. This gives rise to some concern that Australian house prices are overvalued and due for a correction, if not a crash, particularly as unemployment rises and mortgage repayments become too hard for many. Some people could face the prospect of negative equity, where their home loan exceeds the value of their property.

In residential property's favour, many argue there's an undersupply of housing. Demand for housing in many areas seems to be holding up, and our population is growing.

Chapter 12, 'Your castle', looks at the property market and the state of home affordability.

WHY IS AUSTRALIA THE LAST ECONOMY STANDING?

While the financial crisis swept the world, Australia remained among the last developed countries to avoid a technical recession. So far, our government hasn't had to bail out or nationalise banks. But what made us different?

Firstly, the federal government had a number of tools at its disposal to try to stave off recession. At 7.25%, our official interest rate was relatively high, giving the Reserve Bank room to manoeuvre. It cut rates by 4.25% as the downturn hit, bringing the target cash rate down to 3% by mid-2009. More rate cuts are possible. The Reserve Bank's purpose when cutting rates is to make borrowing cheaper, encouraging us to spend and invest more money, stimulating economic growth. That's called monetary policy.

The second major factor in our favour was that our national budget was in surplus, meaning the government had money to spend to stimulate the economy – known in economics as fiscal policy. The billions of dollars in stimulus packages are examples of this fiscal spending policy at work.

Other factors put forward to explain our country's relative good performance are our strong natural resources sector and that we're less reliant on the United States and European Union, where the downturn has been most severe. Asia has been badly impacted by the downturn, but not to the same extent. Australian government regulators also argue that good standards of regulation helped protect our banking system from a similar fate to international financial institutions – so far, the problems have been mild compared to overseas. That said, several of our banks have had some exposure to 'toxic assets' and other bad loans, with several billion dollars of bad debts written off by major banks.

Will our banks survive?

Australian banks have coped with the financial crisis much better than their overseas counterparts, avoiding the need for government bail-outs and managing to stay profitable. Their credit ratings remain high in international terms. In March 2009, the CEO of a major financial institution said that local banks had been managed through the crisis better than foreign investment banks. He added, a little ominously. 'We'll see how they go in the future.'

How will the downturn affect me?

Interestingly, some economists don't pay too much heed to the technical definition of a recession widely quoted in the media. Saul Eslake, ANZ's Chief Economist, says a real recession is where an economy's actual growth is less than its potential growth. 'That's why people in China think they're in a recession despite the fact that their economy is currently growing at 6%, instead of the potential 8%'.

Changes in the unemployment rate – for example, an increase of 1 to 1.5% in less than a year – provide a fair indication that an economy's growth is falling short of its potential. For many people, whether or not Australia has entered a technical recession is irrelevant, because the combination of substantial losses on superannuation savings, rising unemployment and fear about the future are already making people feel and act like they are in one. Unemployment is expected to rise to somewhere between 6% and 9% in the next couple of years – the hundreds of thousands of people who lose jobs in that period will have no doubt that they're in a serious downturn.

Time to bunker down?

Even though most people will keep their jobs, uncertainty about the future is quite rightly affecting our behaviour. It's natural that people are feeling the need to rein-in their spending, save more for the future and generally 'bunker down'. Some people won't be able to avoid redundancy – when it happens, it happens very quickly, as we are already seeing with organisations closing or moving offshore. While you might not be able to avoid a redundancy, you can take steps to reduce the chances that you'll be affected, and think about a plan B.

3

Your personal economy

Is your budget in surplus or deficit? Make sure you spend less than you earn.

We've been hearing a lot about national economies receding and big spending taking their budgets into deficit. Everyone's talking about macroeconomics – stimulus packages, fiscal policies and gross domestic products. But have you given much time to analysing the health of your 'personal economy'?

Before a licensed financial planner can consider giving personal advice, he or she needs to undertake a thorough analysis of the client's present situation. Only after this fact-find can they consider what strategies and products might be appropriate for the client's needs.

The first step on the road to recession-proofing your finances also involves taking an inventory of your current position. Even if you end up seeing a planner for financial advice, the process will be worthwhile and save time later. Also, quite apart from the issue of financial advice, an analysis of the health of your personal economy – an exercise in simple budgeting – will help you decide if you need to cut your spending, and where. Here is a check-list to help you.

A – ASSESS WHAT COMES IN

It should not take too long to calculate exactly how much money you have coming in.

- Your after-tax wages – depending on your circumstances, it may not be appropriate to include bonuses or anticipated pay rises, as they can change
- Income from investments – that might include dividends from shares and term deposit interest
- Other income sources – part-time job.

B – DETERMINE WHAT GOES OUT

Make a detailed list of all the things you spend on. The following websites have comprehensive online budgeting tools: <www.fido.gov.au/calculators>, <www.nicri.org.au> and <www.understanding money.gov.au>. Here are some of the main costs to consider:

- bills: electricity, gas, phone and internet, council rates
- cars: consider the cost of upkeep, repairs and registration and petrol
- charitable donations
- children's expenses
- clothing and footwear
- discretionary items, such as DVDs and books
- education and training
- entertainment and socialising, including movies, shows, dinner parties and going out
- food and groceries
- gyms and sporting clubs
- health costs, including medical bills and consultations, and private health insurance
- home maintenance and improvements
- insurance
- rent
- savings and investments
- takeaway food
- regular loan repayments and interest that you make each month (home, investment, car, personal) and credit card
- transport
- travel and holidays.

IS YOUR PERSONAL ECONOMY IN SURPLUS OR DEFICIT?

So, what was the result of the budgeting exercise? To determine if your cash flow is positive or negative, subtract your expenditure (B) from your income (A).

If you are spending more than comes in

If your personal budget is in deficit – in other words more money is going out than comes in – don't panic. There are some cases when this situation is okay. Governments allow their budgets to go into deficit during a recession (as they invest money to stimulate economic growth – the alternative would be to tax people more and spend less money, which could be counterproductive in tough times). Similarly, there are periods in life when you may need to spend more than you earn. Education, for example, is usually a great long-term investment in yourself that leads to financial and other rewards later, though along the way you might have trouble making ends meet.

But in general, running a personal budget deficit isn't sustainable. As a nation, that's just what consumers were doing before the recession kicked in and we urgently started to save more and spend less. The best thing to do is to seek help – and fast. A financial counsellor can help explain your options.

The other important issue is to look at how you are funding this unsustainable spending pattern. If it's with a credit card, you could run into serious difficulties, with interest rates often around 20%. There are cheaper ways. Go to chapter 13, 'Avoiding a personal credit crunch', for tips on how to get out of debt.

If you are spending less than your income

Hopefully your personal budget is in surplus, though most of us can improve the balance. There are two ways: increase your income or reduce your spending. In a tough economic environment, where people are being laid off left, right and centre, increasing your income is easier said than done. But reducing your spending is within reach for many of us.

The pie chart below shows where Australians, as a whole, direct their cash. Unfortunately, it's from 2003–04; the Australian Bureau of Statistics *Household Spending Survey* hasn't been updated since then. Some of our spending patterns are likely to have changed; a greater proportion of the income of many households is likely to have been directed to interest and principal repayments when interest rates rose, though recent interest rate cuts have eased this problem. The chart gives an idea of the important areas you can look at for clues about where you most need to cut costs. Housing, food, transport and recreation are the main expenses for many families.

Household spending, 2003–04

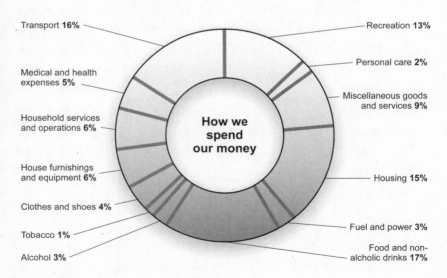

SOURCE Chart generated from ABS Household Expenditure Survey 2003–4

MANDATORY EXPENSES

These are the items that you simply can't avoid spending money on. But while many people think their mandatory expenses are set in stone, there are lots of creative ways that you can pay less for essential products and services. Sometimes it just takes a little creativity and thinking outside the square. Here are a few examples:

- *Electricity and gas* – the best way to cut your power bills is to use less. Implementing energy-saving strategies and habits not only saves you money, but is also good for the environment. And now that we have competing electricity suppliers in several states, you could also benefit by switching your supplier. Chapter 17, 'Slash your household expenses', has more details.

- *Telecommunications* – you might save money by bundling your home phone, mobile and Internet into a package with one provider. You may also cut your expenditure by moving to a plan more suited to your call patterns.

- *Your mortgage* – a major expense for households, but many could be paying less. As long as the exit or set-up fees don't outweigh the benefits, switching home loan provider could reap big benefits. Another option is to threaten to leave your lender to bargain for a better rate, or to switch to your present lender's no frills loan. Look at chapter 14, 'The mortgage meltdown' for more tips.

- *Food* – a huge amount of the food we buy is wasted, and we also get sucked in to purchasing groceries we don't really need. There are simple ways that we can all cut our weekly grocery spend and help the bottom line – check out chapter 16, 'Slash your shopping bills', for our advice.

Don't try to do everything at once – chances are you'll find it all too hard and just give up. Think about ways to cut your expenses one at a time.

SET mini goals

DISCRETIONARY EXPENSES

This is where many of us can make big savings. This doesn't have to mean being a Scrooge and having no fun. It's more about prioritising what you feel is really worth spending money on, and to some degree, reining-in your spending so that treats are occasional things, rather than everyday events.

It's important to do what works for you, but here are some ideas:

- *'Pay yourself'* a set amount from each wage packet that you're allowed to spend on discretionary items. Try not to exceed that budget.
- *Set small goals and work towards them.* For example, this week or month you might decide to look at ways to reduce energy use around the home, next month check out whether you're on the best phone plan and the following month plan to look at ways to reduce your home insurance expenses. It's all about working towards these goals to save money without any loss of utility.
- *Prioritise what's worth spending money on.* For some people, a gym membership and pay TV subscription is worth the $2000 per year it could cost. Others could take it or leave it. Do the sums to find out where your money is going and decide what's worth keeping.
- *Save money on everyday expenses.* If you save say $5 a day by bringing a sandwich to work and save another $3 by cutting out takeaway coffees on the way in the morning, you would have cut your expenses by another $2000 over a year.
- *You don't have to stop doing the things you enjoy.* You might be an avid reader, for example, but have you checked out your local public library as an alternative to buying $25 paperbacks?
- *Pay your bills when they arrive* – even if they're not due for three weeks, you can schedule the payment for a future date with Internet banking. That way you'll avoid exorbitant late payment fees and know that you're up-to-date with your payments.

Beware of 'lifestyle inflation', where you use a pay rise or bonus to fund a more lavish lifestyle instead of spending the same as before, and saving the extra income.

SMART

ASSESS YOUR ASSETS AND LIABILITIES

An important part of your stocktake is to assess the assets and liabilities (debts) you currently have, to determine the health of your 'personal balance sheet'. This is vital for identifying the borrowings that you should focus on reducing, setting investment goals, understanding your own needs and filling any gaps. It can't replace the professional advice a licensed financial planner could provide, but it will help determine if your debts are under control; if you have a well-balanced and diversified investment portfolio and adequate insurance coverage.

Your assets are everything you own – this could include cars, your home, its contents, your investments, money in the bank, shares, your income and superannuation. Your liabilities are what you owe – the remaining balance of your mortgage, credit card and other debts are usually the most significant liabilities most people have.

Assuming your liabilities outweigh your assets, and you have dependents, you may need to ensure you have adequate life and income protection insurance just in case you become sick and are unable to work, or worse. Chapter 18 on life and income protection insurance gives pointers on how to work out your needs.

During this recession, which has been induced by the bursting of a major debt bubble, many of us will need to do all we can to improve and repair the health of our personal balance sheets. The most obvious way is to pay off more debt (mortgages and credit cards) and increase our savings.

Greed is not good

With the recession starting to bite we could well see a return to old-fashioned concepts like saving and thrift, which for some people seem to have been lost in the heady days of a credit and spending binge.

Nick Foley, Managing Director of the brand consultancy Landor Associates, thinks the era of conspicuous consumption is over – for now. 'Public displays of wealth are not appropriate in this economic environment,' Foley says. 'People are acting like they're in a recession, saving more and moving away from "aspirational" brands and goods like Louis Vuiton and Porsche, even if they can afford them. This is similar to the early 1990s, when there was a shift away from the crassness of the eighties, as depicted by Michael Douglas's character in the movie *Wall Street*, who proclaimed that greed is good. It's a cyclical thing – people aren't changing their tastes for altruistic reasons – we'll see the rise of consumerism and greed again.'

4

Comparing investments

'37% of investors don't have a long-term financial goal or a plan to reach it.' – ASIC, 2008 Investor Survey

Before rushing into investments, it's important to know what you're trying to achieve with your money. This means setting goals and then deciding on an investment strategy for achieving them. Your goals may be short-term – for example, to put money aside each week to pay for a holiday. Or, you might have a medium-term aim of saving enough for a house deposit within the next five years. A long-term goal might be much more ambitious – to build up enough super to retire comfortably, or to have your mortgage paid off in 15 years' time.

The investment approaches suitable for each of these objectives will differ. That's why goal setting is really important. In fact, you might well be working towards three different goals like these at the same time. The short-term target might require an investment that's safe (if you know you'll need the money to pay for a holiday next year you wouldn't want to risk losing it), flexible (allowing you to add additional savings when you have them), liquid (meaning you can actually get your money back within a year) and ideally providing a return that beats inflation. But with the five-year savings plan for a house deposit, you wouldn't be so restricted. You'd still want to know that your money plus interest is ready to use in five years, but you won't need to withdraw it at short notice and you may be willing to accept some volatility of performance along the way.

MATCHING YOUR NEEDS WITH YOUR INVESTMENTS

So how do you go about finding the right mix of investments for your circumstances? A licensed financial planner should be able to help you. Otherwise, some of the issues to consider are:

- *Your risk tolerance* – this means your willingness to accept the potential for volatility and investment losses in the expectation of higher returns. There's usually a direct relationship between risk and expected return. The more risk you take, the greater the return you should expect in order to compensate you for taking the risk. Conversely, if you want certainty about your returns (low risk), you're going to have to settle for lower returns. There's more about the risks with investments later in this chapter (page 34).

- *Diversification* – the most basic way to spread risk is to divide your money among good quality investments in different assets classes (such as bonds, cash deposits, shares and property). Don't put all your eggs in one basket – this intensifies the risk that you'll lose everything if something goes wrong.

- *Timeframe* – how long do you want to invest for? 'Growth' investments like shares can be good long-term investments, but in the short-term there will be ups and downs (volatility) and the likelihood of losing money in some years. For that reason, shares are usually unsuitable short-term investments for novice investors, especially if you know you'll need to withdraw the money in a year or two. While they may perform well and give you a big profit in that timeframe, shares may also decline in value leaving you worse off. For most people, financial advisers usually recommend a minimum timeframe of 5 to 7 years for share investments.

- *Liquidity* – this just means how easily and quickly you can access your money. Perhaps the least liquid investment going is superannuation – if you make an extra contribution to your fund now, you're unlikely to be able to access it until you retire. A mortgage fund that issues a freeze on withdrawals is another non-liquid investment. On the other hand, a bank deposit account is extremely liquid – if you want to withdraw money, you just have to put your card in an ATM.

- *Income or capital growth?* – some investments are designed to provide a regular income; others won't give you regular payments but will hopefully grow in value over time. Term deposits have been a popular income investment, though that's likely to reduce as interest rates have been cut to their lowest levels in decades. Even so, lots of assets can provide income. Some shares, for example, consistently pay good dividends, which can be a solid source of income for shareholders. Other companies retain most of their earnings to invest in company growth, which the shareholders hope will be reflected in long-term increases in the share price.

- *How to beat inflation* – inflation just means the rate at which the prices of goods and services we buy is increasing. For investors, it's often said that inflation is the enemy, because if you don't earn more from an investment than the rate of inflation, you're losing money in 'real' terms. The money you invest today will buy fewer goods and services, if its return in a year's time doesn't keep pace with the rate of inflation.

Start to think about short-, medium- and long-term goals to aim for. Then figure out – or get help to figure out – a plan to make them happen.

Do this NOW

RISK PROFILES OF DIFFERENT INVESTMENTS

The return you expect from an investment should compensate for the level of risk you're taking. The attributes of the main asset classes:

- *Australian government bonds* – These should be very safe. In the past, governments in countries like Argentina and Mexico have defaulted on their repayments, but this seems highly unlikely in a country like Australia. Summary: low-risk, low expected return, though domestic bonds have been the top performers during the financial crisis (see page 75).

- *Bank deposits* – These are low-risk, if the bank is an Authorised Deposit Taking Institution (ADI), because in 2008 the Australian government guaranteed deposits of up to $1 million in those institutions for three years. (Larger deposits are also guaranteed, but they attract a deposit guarantee fee.) The money you invest should be safe, though in the present low-interest rate environment you won't earn much of an additional return. Summary: low-risk, low expected return.

- *Managed funds* – Depending on where the money is invested and the company running the fund, these funds range from safe government bond and fixed interest funds, to risky hedge funds and equity funds. Summary: they range from low- to high-risk, and so the expected returns vary too.

- *Property* – This may be in the form of direct property (for example, your home or an investment unit), or a Real Estate Investment Trust (REIT). While Australian residential property has cooled and declined in value a bit recently, it hasn't had the 20% falls of the US and UK. We look at some of the possibilities and risks with residential property in chapter 12, 'Your Castle'. Commercial property trusts (managed funds that invest in commercial property) have had a very bad time, however, losing up to 50% of their value in 2008. Check out chapter 7 on 'Managed funds' for more information. Summary: commercial property trusts can have high volatility and risk, and the potential for significant capital gains or losses too.

- *Unrated debentures, notes and mortgage funds* – While some of the companies offering these investments continue to promise 'fixed interest' returns above 8%, their advertisements include warnings about investment risks. Summary: investors risk not getting some or all of their interest and capital back; advertised investment returns are moderate.

- *Shares* – Company shares are volatile investments whose value can fluctuate wildly in a short space of time. In the past shares have provided Australian investors with good capital growth and returns, though November 2007 saw the beginning of one of our biggest share market falls. Summary: at the higher end of the risk and volatility spectrum.

INVESTMENT RISKS AND THE GLOBAL FINANCIAL CRISIS

So what are the main risks to consider with investment strategies and products? Overleaf are ten risks and their impacts on investors during the global financial crisis (GFC). It's difficult to eliminate risk, but by understanding it you can factor it into your investment decisions.

A CHECKLIST OF TEN RISKS TO CONSIDER

1 *Liquidity risk* – an investment can't be easily converted to cash. GFC example: when the crisis hit, some Australian mortgage funds put a temporary freeze on investors withdrawing their money.

2 *Manager risk* – changes in a company's personnel or management. For example, the manager of an investment fund resigns, casting doubt over future strategies or talent at the fund manager. GFC example: According to investment researcher Morningstar, the resignation of a senior manager at organisations like Colonial First State and Platinum Asset Management in 2009 have been significant events in the industry.

3 *Inflation risk* – investments do not keep pace with the rising price of goods and services. GFC example: If interest rates continue to fall and inflation picks up, investors could be left with lower 'real' returns from their savings and investments.

4 *Legislative risk* – government changes to rules and regulations. GFC example: Changes to superannuation law make it less advantageous to certain investors; the guarantee on bank deposits not being extended to managed funds makes them less attractive and comparatively riskier.

5 *Economic risk* – Impact of national or global economic changes on investments. GFC example: the world economic recession has caused investments in shares and property to plummet.

For an excellent analysis of the trade off between risks and returns, go to <www.fpa.asn.au>. To see the riskiness of each investment category, check out the 'risk meters' at the website of the National Information Centre on Retirement Investments <www.nicri.org.au>.

6   *Illegal activity* – investment losses due to fraud. GFC example: in the US, Bernard Madoff was jailed in 2009 after confessing to one of the biggest frauds in history, a Ponzi investment scheme of epic proportions that led to huge investor losses.

7   *Timing risk* – entering and exiting the market at a good or bad time. GFC example: A basket of Australian shares bought in November 2007 lost up to 50% by March 2009. And if you sold the shares at that point, you would have missed the 25% increase that was achieved by June.

8   *Currency risk* – changes in the value of foreign currency. GFC example: the Australian dollar's depreciation against the US dollar in 2008 means that Australians who made offshore investments may have benefited from exchange rate movements.

9   *Major event risk* – man-made or naturally occurring events that produce a shock to the system. GFC example: the US sub-prime mortgage crisis eventually led to events that decimated investment markets and gave rise to 'The Great Recession'.

10 *Diversification risk* – A poorly diversified investment portfolio intensifies the chance of losing money. GFC example: if the option you chose for superannuation only invests in shares, you would have seen huge declines. If you had been diversified between safe and speculative investments, the losses wouldn't have been quite as bad.

Risk/return mismatches

It's often said that the greater the risk, the greater the return. This is not quite accurate, because the truth is that the greater the risk, the greater the return *you should expect*. Sometimes there's a mismatch between these two factors. Take, for example, some of the unlisted and unrated debentures and mortgage funds that went bust in the last five years. The risks with those investments were extremely high – there was a real chance that investors could lose most or all of the money they'd invested, and not receive the interest promised either – and that's exactly what happened. Yet despite taking these huge risks, investors were only being promised a return of somewhere between 7% and 10%. That was only a few per cent more than rock-solid safe-as-houses bank deposits were paying. Clearly, the risk of these mortgage fund and debenture investments bore little relation to the return – it was a total mismatch. Investors who relied on the maxim that advertised return indicates the level of risk were badly stung and let down.

Rebalancing act

It's important to review your investments at least annually, to check that the mix of assets still suits your needs and risk profile. After a strong share market gains or a 'bear' market (when prices decline by 20% or more), changes in the value of your investments could leave you with more or less risk than you really want.

LISA'S PORTFOLIO

Lisa invested 30% of her portfolio in safe cash deposits and 70% in shares in 2003. She left her investments untouched during that period. By mid 2007, Lisa's portfolio had grown by 77%, thanks mainly to the great share market performance during that time (average annualised growth of 19%, versus 5% for cash). However, at the end of the four years the make-up of her investment portfolio had changed, with a higher proportion in shares (79%) compared to when the investments were made in 2003.

When the share market crashed at the end of 2007, Lisa was more susceptible than if she had rebalanced her portfolio back to its original 70%/30% weightings.

5

Defensive plays

*Park short-term
savings in a safe place for
a competitive return.*

In the years leading up to the financial crash, the money we were putting aside for a rainy day declined dramatically, to the extent that when it started to rain – and then *pour* – some people were caught out with little shelter.

In the 1970s households saved up to 15% of their disposable income. By the mid–1980s the rate was down to around 10% and during the mid–1990s people were saving just 5% of their spare money. By 2002 the downward trend had continued to such an extent that we entered *negative* savings territory.

Put simply, as a nation, we stopped saving. While the statistics show that our overall household 'wealth', driven by the share and property markets, increased in the first seven years of this decade, in 2007, a report for the Investments and Financial Services Association by The Allen Consulting Group confirmed that household saving had virtually collapsed and that 'a full-blown household debt binge' was underway.

As we come to terms with the traumatic economic events of the last eighteen months and brace ourselves for the possibility of more bad news, we're seeing a return to old-fashioned concepts like saving and thrift. By 2009, the savings rate was heading back towards 7% and predicted to continue to grow. Fear and uncertainty about the future could be the main motivators for this change – particularly as unemployment is rising and superannuation and investment losses have hit home. People are seeing the need to build up their safety net – and fast.

THE FLIGHT TO SAFETY

In turbulent economic times, we have a natural tendency to shift our money to conservative investments. And while putting too much of your money into low-risk investments may limit what you can earn in the medium- to long-term, there's a place for conservative options in most balanced portfolios.

At various points in time, professional investors use cash to create or just protect wealth. In late 2007, if you had shifted your investments to cash at fixed interest and away from shares or property, your investments would be worth about 30% more than someone who remained in 'growth' assets during the same period. Not losing money and even earning a little is a much better result than losing 20% of your wealth.

But hindsight is a wonderful thing. Whether you should shift to cash and fixed interest now is a different decision, which shouldn't be taken lightly. Your asset allocation should ideally be aligned with your investment profile, with your timeframe being a key consideration.

Remember, deposit (cash) accounts and fixed interest investments can be safe, but at present, their interest rates are unlikely to beat inflation, which by 2009 was running at about 2.5% per annum. So

The government guarantee

The federal government followed many of its overseas counterparts by guaranteeing the safety of deposits with Authorised Deposit-taking Institutions (ADIs), which are banks, building societies and credit unions. The guarantee is for the first $1 million of deposits held with an ADI, which covers the vast majority of deposits held in Australia. So if a bank went down the tubes, your savings would be repaid by the government, unless of course the government was unable to honour this commitment.

In the last 50 years, governments of some countries such as Argentina, Mexico and Russia have been unable to repay their debts. These problems were due to very large debts owed to overseas creditors, and which did not affect domestic depositors. It seems highly unlikely that this would happen in Australia. You might wonder why a government in debt couldn't just print more money to pay off what it owes. That is a last resort – but printing money can lead to high inflation and serious economic problems. The disastrous consequences of recklessly printing money can be seen in Zimbabwe where the result was inflation increasing at thousands of percentage points.

ADIs include all banks, building societies and credit unions that are regulated by the Australian Prudential Regulation Authority (APRA). Managed funds and other types of investments aren't covered by the guarantee scheme because they aren't supervised by APRA.

The guarantee applies for a period of three years (until October 2011) and for savings up to $1 million per person; for larger deposits, an insurance fee applies. To ensure you're saving with an ADI, check the list at <www.apra.gov.au>.

after income tax at your marginal rate is deducted from the interest you earn, money in a deposit account could be losing value in 'real' terms.

Regardless, everyone needs a safe place for at least some of their money, for day-to-day expenses and short-term needs. Many of us need a 'buffer' of cash, available at short notice for unforeseen events and expenses. These days an emergency fund is a good idea. Stuffing money under the mattress isn't the answer and the interest paid on most banks' transaction accounts is paltry, so you're better off shifting short-term savings elsewhere. Let's consider your options, which include:

- Online savings accounts
- Term deposits
- Traditional savings accounts
- Cash management accounts
- Government bonds, perhaps the safest investments, are discussed in chapter 7.

Term deposits

Term deposits offered by banks, building societies and credit unions provide a safe haven for short- to medium-term investments. Of course, safety comes at a price. While term deposits paying 8% were available up to early 2008, rates declined significantly in the second half of the year, following the Reserve Bank's cash rate cuts. By mid-2009 the best one-year interest rate you'll get is about 4%.

When you open a term deposit, you're locking away that money for a set period of time. It can't be touched until the term expires – unless you pay a hefty break fee. So only invest money that you won't need in the near future.

Interest may be paid out each month or year, providing investors with an income, albeit a small one in the current low-interest rate environment. Otherwise, you can choose to have the interest earned added to your term deposit balance so that it too will start to accrue interest, leaving you with more money at maturity.

Online saving accounts

High-interest-Internet savings accounts provide another good option for the short-term. Promises of 'no bank fees ever' coupled with competitive rates paved the way about five years ago, changing the way many of us save. In the last few years, the interest paid on online savers has rivalled term deposits, but without the same restrictions. Unlike term deposits, your money can be withdrawn any time, with no fee.

Usually, you link your day-to-day transaction account to the online saver, transferring money between the accounts whenever you like. Typically, the online savings account has no fees, but is very restricted too with no facilities such as an ATM card, bill payment option or chequebook, for example.

Over the last five years, institutions such as BankWest and ING Direct have been consistently competitive in this category. Thankfully, that forced their larger competitors to pull up their socks and offer better rates; the major banks now all have decent online savings accounts as well. The Dutch-owned Rabobank also entered the market with competitive rates, as did credit unions, which can offer very good deals. You can check the latest rates at <www.ratecity.com.au> or <www.infochoice.com.au>.

One thing to watch out for is the way in which interest is advertised. Sometimes the eye-catching headline rate only applies for a period of time, such as the first year. Then your interest drops to the standard rate.

Do this NOW

Check that the high interest rate is calculated on the account's daily balance, even in months when you make a withdrawal or don't add anything to the account. Interest is usually credited (compounded) to the account monthly.

If your transaction account pays low interest, consider an online saver for short-term savings. They don't charge fees so there's really nothing to lose – and there's much better interest to be earned. $5000 in an account paying 4% interest would earn more than $200 per year. Some transaction accounts are paying less than a dollar per year for the same balance.

CASE STUDY
SAFETY FIRST FOR DAVE

Dave, who is in his thirties, likes to put all his spare money into his online savings account and extra home loan repayments. He's risk-averse and hates the thought of investing his hard-earned cash in shares. 'With a savings account, I know my money will be there tomorrow. With shares, there's the chance I could lose everything,' he says. 'So I put the money into the savings account because there's a $10,000 per year limit on the extra repayments off the principal that I can make to my fixed rate mortgage. When the fixed rate home loan ends my plan is to put any extra money from the savings account onto my mortgage.'

Dave's present online account is with ING Direct, which is paying a rate of 3.5% per annum at June 2009. That's not bad in the current environment – and like other banks the money is government-guaranteed. However, Dave could earn another 0.50% with a range of online savings accounts from banks that are also government-guaranteed. If his average balance is $10000 switching could earn Dave an extra $50 per year. It's not all that much, but every little bit helps (put all the tips in this book together and you could save much more). See the Appendix for where to check the latest rates, which are constantly changing.

Cash management accounts (CMAs)

These are designed for both transaction and saving purposes. They usually combine a decent interest rate with the facility to withdraw from ATMs, pay bills and write cheques. CMAs often require a starting balance of several thousand dollars. Interest rates are usually lower than online savings accounts, but better than standard transaction accounts which usually pay little or no interest.

It may not seem like an 'investment', but if you have a home loan, putting extra cash into it will provide one of the best long-term, low-risk returns around. Go to chapter 14, 'The mortgage meltdown', for the simple ways you can fast-track your mortgage to save thousands in interest and take years off your loan.

INVEST IN your home loan

Regular savings accounts

'Bonus saver' accounts often have two interest rate tiers, with reasonable interest being paid if you make a certain minimum monthly contribution each month and don't make withdrawals. In months when you don't satisfy those conditions, a lower (sometimes paltry) rate of interest is paid.

One advantage of bonus saver accounts is that they encourage you to make regular savings, the higher interest rate being your incentive. But if you are disciplined and save regularly anyway, another account such as a good online saver may pay similar interest without penalising you in months when you don't make a contribution. Compare and check out the interest rates and conditions.

Capital protected investments

Generally this is a type of managed fund, rather than a deposit account, so the government deposit guarantee doesn't apply. These funds, which usually invest in a range of growth assets such as shares, provide a guarantee that in some cases if investment markets perform poorly investors will get back at least what they originally invested. If markets perform well, higher returns are possible. So, what is the catch? You might invest your money for a period of a few years and get no growth or additional return, which means you could lose money after inflation is taken into account. And, the guarantee may not apply in some cases.

Expect to see more of these investments being launched, as nervous investors wonder where to put their money without risking too much. Read the Product Disclosure Statements for the full story, including the catches.

First Home Saver Accounts: a special case

If you're saving a deposit for your first home, a First Home Saver Account (FHSA) can be a great option. The FHSA scheme was launched by the federal government in October 2008 to help people break into the property market. Essentially, the government will match what you contribute to the account with a free 17% co-contribution, up to an annual limit of $850. And the interest paid by your account provider (mostly banks, building societies and credit unions) will be taxed at 15%, a lower tax rate than most people pay on their savings, which are taxed at your marginal income tax rate.

For the right people, the FHSA can be a great scheme. If you're at least four years away from buying your first home, consider them as a way to save for your deposit.

However, there are a number of significant traps to be aware of before committing:

- You must contribute at least $1000 in at least four separate financial years. The years don't have to be consecutive.
- The proceeds of the account can only be used to buy or build your first home.

- If you close the account for any other reason, the balance is transferred to your super fund (so in most cases, you won't be able to access the money until you retire).
- There will be a delay before the government contribution is added to your account each year, as this can't happen until you submit your income tax return for the year and the financial institution reports your FHSA savings to the Tax Office.

CHOICE produced a guide to choosing a fair, transparent account with low fees and competitive interest. For details on how the banks and others measure up against key benchmarks, as well as all the info you need to know about the scheme, go to <www.choice.com.au/money>.

DEBENTURES, NOTES AND MORTGAGE FUNDS: A WARNING

8% to 10% fixed and secured annual interest is a pretty tempting offer, isn't it? It could be pretty risky too.

In the present low-interest environment, with central bank rates drifting under 3%, some investors may be attracted to investments offering much higher 'fixed' rates. They include debentures, secured and unsecured notes, and mortgage funds. By mid-2009, some of these companies were advertising annual returns to investors of more than double what government-guaranteed banks were paying.

We're likely to see some of these investments become more prominent during the downturn, as investors look for a better paying alternative to bank deposits. But many of these mortgage funds, debentures and notes have not been independently assessed by a credit rating agency, so investors don't have an independent evaluation of the risks or quality of the investment. And the risks with some of these investments are significant. They often use investors' money to invest and lend it to property developers, for mortgages, and for

Avoiding penalty fees

Penalty fees charged by banks, building societies and credit unions can be an unnecessary drain on your finances. They include the $30 fee you're charged when a cheque you write bounces (or worse still, when a cheque that you lodge to your account is dishonoured), or the penalty imposed on you when a direct debit is dishonoured by your bank because you've insufficient funds. Your priority should be to avoid these fees, but if you happen to get stung, you can appeal it with your financial institution. CHOICE and the Consumer Action Law Centre have been running a campaign to get these penalties overturned – in many cases, consumers have had them successfully reversed. Go to <www.fairfees.com.au> for information on how to argue your case.

Another way to reduce your banking costs is to avoid using other financial institutions and companies' ATMs, as you'll be charged a 'foreign' ATM fee. Stick to using your own bank, building society or credit unions machines if you can. It's worth contacting your institution to check the cheapest way to use your everyday account and make cash withdrawals.

construction projects. But if they're able to pay you 9%, they must be charging the borrowers significantly higher interest. With tough business conditions – particularly in the property and construction sectors – there's a chance that some borrowers will default on their repayments, placing investors' money at increased risk.

A number of high-profile collapses in this fixed interest sector, which includes investment companies without credit ratings, have occurred in the last three years. That was at a time when business conditions generally were better and interest rates were high. We weren't in a recession when companies like Australian Capital Reserve, Westpoint, Bridgecorp Finance and Fincorp collapsed. Investors have lost hundreds of millions of dollars. CHOICE has been contacted by desperate people who realised that their substantial investments – which were often tens of thousands of dollars – are unlikely to be recovered.

The advertising and disclosure rules for these funds have been greatly improved by Australian Securities and Investments Commission (ASIC), so you can have a better idea of the risks. For example, the small print in an advertisement for one mortgage fund offering over 9% in February 2009 stated:

'[The investment] is not a bank deposit and carries the risk of investors achieving lower than expected returns or not getting all or part of the principal back.'

UNLISTED and UNRATED investments

- *Never invest in an unlisted and unrated debenture, mortgage fund or promissory note without understanding the risks. A higher promised return means a higher risk that you won't get your money back.*
- *Read the PDS and check whether the company or fund meet ASIC's safety benchmarks. Most fail at least one.*
- *Know that these investments aren't comparable to safe investments like bank deposits.*
- *Bear in mind that investors have lost hundreds of millions of dollars when unrated and unlisted debentures, notes and mortgage funds collapsed.*

SAFETY CHECKS

If you're considering a fixed interest investment that promises to pay much more than banks, check out whether it meets ASIC's eight benchmarks. This will help you understand the risks and decide whether you still want to invest your money. For mortgage funds, for example, the following must be disclosed:

ASIC BENCHMARKS FOR UNLISTED AND UNRATED MORTGAGE FUNDS

- *Liquidity* – Does the fund have enough cash and liquid assets to meet its obligations to you and other investors?
- *Borrowing* – How much money has the fund borrowed, and will it be able to pay its debts falling due in the next year?
- *Diversification* – Does the fund spread its risks by lending to different loans, borrowers and investments?
- *Related party transactions* – Will your money, or other money held by the mortgage fund, be lent to organisations and individuals that are related to the fund? If the answer is yes, this may imply greater risks.
- *Valuations* – How does the fund value its underlying assets, such as property and mortgages?
- *Loan to value ratios* – How much money will the fund lend compared to the value of the security for the loan?
- *Distributions* – Where is the money paid to you coming from and is this sustainable?
- *Withdrawals* – Can you take your money out of the fund and how long will withdrawals take?

Each pooled mortgage fund needs to disclose how it performs for each of these benchmarks. Even if it passes all of the benchmarks, this doesn't imply your money is safe. By the same token, if a mortgage fund fails one or more of the benchmarks, this doesn't guarantee it will lose money. However, the benchmarks give you an indication of the risks.

As CHOICE said in 2006, before the collapse of a number of unrated debenture and mortgage funds, professional investors wouldn't touch some of these investments. Shouldn't you be equally discerning with your money?

6

Investing in shares

Maximising potential returns
for the medium- and long-term

Conservative and safe investments have a place in every balanced portfolio, but the after-tax returns they provide may not even keep pace with inflation. So in real terms, you could lose money. That's why investors look to growth investments – such as shares (equities) – for a decent return over the medium- to long-term.

Recent events have left nobody doubting that shares are risky and their value is volatile – expect further ups and downs, particularly in the short-term. Neither this chapter, nor even this book, is aimed at 'day traders' – who try to take advantage of dramatic short-term rises and falls in share prices. However, depending on your objectives, timeframe and appetite for risk, shares may have a place in your long-term investment plans.

When you invest in a company's shares, you become a part-owner in the company, with the right to vote at AGMs. But of course the main reason to buy shares is to try to make money. Shares may appreciate in value over time, enabling you to sell them later at a profit. Shares can also provide you with a regular income, when companies pay dividends to their investors. We'll look at the type of shares that are suitable for income or capital growth later.

CRASH, BANG, WALLOP

After four years of almost 20% annual growth, 2008 was one of the worst on record for share market investors. Stock markets crashed worldwide. In Australia, the S&P/ASX 200, which represents the market value of our biggest and best companies, declined from around 6680 points in November 2007 to as low as 3250 in March 2008, a 50% decline and the lowest point for five years. (The value of a share index is expressed in points, a measure of the value of all companies on the index, usually weighted so that movements in large companies' share prices have a bigger effect than those of smaller companies).

And as their investors are painfully aware, some of the individual stocks' blow-ups were even more spectacular. In the space of two years, Macquarie Group had highs of $98 and lows of $15 and by June 2009 was around $30. Babcock and Brown fell from its $28 high to be trading at just 22 cents by December 2008, a loss of 93%. Other companies that had lost more than 90% of their value by October 2008 included such names as ABC Learning Centres (–94%), Allco Finance (–98%) and Centro Properties (– 98%).

There's little doubt that investors are hurting. Share portfolios have plummeted. Many people who borrowed money to invest in shares (margin loans) when the going was good have received 'margin' calls – when the bank demands you repay at least some of the loan, which can involve selling shares at a loss to recoup money.

The million dollar question is: 'Where to from here?' If you have a share portfolio, the last thing you'd want to do is sell at the 'bottom' of the market. But it's difficult, if not impossible, to know if and when the market is going to start a path of growth again – as the saying goes, 'nobody rings a bell to let investors know the market has bottomed-out'. Even the professionals find it almost impossible to time the top and bottom of markets, and few saw the crash coming.

HISTORICAL TRENDS

Firstly, a disclaimer that you should see in almost every investment advertisement: Past performance is NOT an indication of future returns! However, looking at what's happened before can help us learn about the trends.

- Over the long-term, Australian share markets have increased in value and the general trend is upwards.
- Strong increases in share values can happen quite quickly. For example, in the strong 'bull' run (when investors are buying shares and they're rising in value) from March 2003 to its high in November 2007, the Australian share market more than doubled in value, increasing by 158%.
- Market collapses and 'bear' markets happen very swiftly too. In November 2007, the Australian market reached an all-time high. Just a year later, the index had halved in value.
- It can take a long time for share markets to recover after a collapse. For example, Aussie shares didn't recover from the 1987 crash until the mid-1990s and some overseas markets have never recovered from crashes – this is a warning against complacency when it comes to shares.
- Overall index charts indicate how the basket of hundreds of companies' share values fared. Of course, some shares were 'dogs' and others were 'stars'. Selecting the right shares is the tricky part.
- While long-term trends have been upwards, how many of us have an investment timeframe of 20, 30 or 50 years?

We can only speculate about where the market will go from here. There's a body of opinion that nobody really knows and that share markets are very unpredictable. Could markets go lower? Absolutely. But by having a portion of your investment portfolio exposed to shares, you'll be in a position to catch potential upswings in the market if and when they happen.

TAKING A LONG-TERM VIEW

Selecting your appropriate mix of investments is dependent on a range of criteria that differ for each individual. One of the key considerations is your investment timeframe. If you have got money to invest now, but you'll need to withdraw it in a year, then shares are almost certainly the wrong option. They are risky and volatile – meaning that what you invest today could be worth much less twelve months down the track. You could get lucky and your shares could be worth much more in a year too – but if you know you will need the money at that point in time, the volatility is probably too great a risk. And if you are investing all your money in just one company's shares, or a small basket of shares, that potential risk and volatility is intensified.

Short-term share investing also adds to your costs such as the brokerage fees you'll pay each time you buy and sell, and tax on any capital gains you make.

For these reasons, financial advisers often recommend a five- to seven-year minimum timeframe for investing in shares. Investment guru Warren Buffett's preferred timeframe is 'forever'. By investing in good companies for the long-term, you increase your chances of riding out the peaks and troughs in the expectation of returns (see the section 'Can you time the markets?' on page 57).

How would you cope with volatility and losses?

Here is a simple question the answer to which might help you determine if you've researched a share purchase adequately, whether you're comfortable with its potential volatility and if you're clear on your investment timeframe and expectations.

QUESTION

You've decided on a share that you want to buy today. What would you do if its price dropped by 10% next week?

ANSWER

A Sell it – I wouldn't be comfortable with that loss.

B Buy some more shares at the new lower price – that would represent even better value.

C Do nothing – I don't mind what happens in the short-term because I believe the share will increase in the long-run.

If you answered A you should probably reconsider buying the share today, particularly in the volatile market we're experiencing. If you can't cope with short-term share price declines, perhaps stable investments are more appropriate. If you answered B or C you're probably comfortable with the investment, its long-term value and its potential volatility.

WARNING: CONVENTIONAL WISDOM IS SOMETIMES WRONG

In the last couple of years, the investment industry has explained away our recent stock market crash by saying shares are a long-term investment and that short-term ups and downs are to be expected. Stay the course and don't panic, they caution.

But are they correct in saying that over the long-term, share markets always rise? Well, we know that the Australian market has done well over the very long term. In fact, for investors, Australian shares have been close to the most profitable in the world over the last one hundred years. But some of the experiences in major overseas markets after crashes tell a different story. The Eureka Report, an excellent online financial newsletter, looked at what happened after three major crashes that are being compared to our recent downturn. It found that economies and markets can take many years to recover from crashes and recessions – that's if they recover at all:

- *1929 crash and 1930s US depression* – After falling by 90% between 1929 and 1932, the market rallied by 111% in 1932 (which still left the market 80% lower than its 1929 high). Over the next ten years, the US market had some serious rallies and subsequent declines (including five bull runs averaging over 90% each time). But by the early 1940s, the market was still at its 1932 level, which means that there were no capital gains for long-term 'buy and hold' investors during the decade.

- *1970s oil shock and bear market* – Just like the 1930s, the 1970s finished roughly where they started. After the oil shock of the early 1970s, the market fell 55%, bottoming in 1975. Two major rallies (53% and 35%) followed, but those gains were wiped out by subsequent declines during the 1970s, before the bull market of 1980–81.

- *1990s Japan's depression and economic crises* – The Japanese Nikkei fell from 40,000 to 15,000 points (63%) between December 1989 and June 1992. Eighteen years later, the index was still around

15,000 points, having experienced some big ups and downs in the meantime. Between 2000 and 2003 the market halved again, dropping below 8000. By 2009 the index was around the same level as the mid 1980s.

So these experiences show that it can take a long time for markets to reach former heights and to start to provide a capital return (1930s and 1970s US markets). In the meantime there may be violent ups and downs. A 'buy and hold' approach wouldn't have been a good strategy in these periods. And the Japanese experience shows that it's simply not true to say that share markets always rise over ten- and twenty-year periods, both considered long terms by any investment professional's standards.

Could the Australian market take a similarly long time to regain its 2007 highs? Is there a chance it'll never recover to those levels in the foreseeable future, just like Japan? With stock markets, *anything* is possible. Nevertheless, many financial advisers and commentators remain optimistic about the long-term future for Australian shares, which they recommend should continue to form a portion of your balanced investment portfolio. And remember, shares can provide a regular income too, even while their price growth is stagnant. The section on income investing has more about this.

ARE SHARES NOW CHEAP?

The graph on page 57 shows the decline in the ratio between Australian shares' prices (P) and company earnings (E), between 2003 and early 2009. In 2004, this 'PE ratio' was as high as 20, meaning shares' prices were twenty times what the companies were earning in profits. By early 2009, PE ratios, on average, are closer to ten. Some commentators see this as indicating a good buying opportunity for long-term investors.

Decline in price/earnings ratios: Are shares now good value?

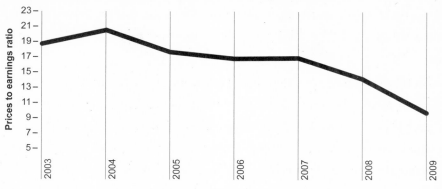

SOURCE The Reserve Bank of Australia Statistics, January 2009

A word of warning – ratios like price/earnings are just an indicator of the present situation, but they don't tell you what will happen in the future. At the time of writing the 'E' part of the price–earnings equation is under pressure, with some experts predicting company earnings could decline by 25% or more. Declining earnings could negatively impact on share prices and growth.

CAN YOU TIME THE MARKETS?

To get the very best returns from shares, you'd trade regularly, buying low and selling high, taking advantage of the dramatic fluctuations in prices. That's what professional traders do every day, often doing trades worth hundreds of thousands of dollars each time.

But can an individual investor have similar success? Well, it's not impossible, but it's extremely unlikely. Stock markets can rise and fall very quickly (the All Ordinaries index fell 42% in just one month – October 1987), but timing the markets is notoriously difficult. Unlike a professional trader working for an investment bank or stockbroking firm, you won't have a team of analysts and economists providing you with up-to-the-minute market reports and research. In other words, the odds are stacked against novice 'day traders'. Also, buying and selling shares regularly has transaction costs, which will eat away at your profits.

Warren Buffett is one of the world's foremost share investment gurus. One of his most famous quotes is: 'It's time in the markets, not market timing, that counts.' (see Warren Buffet's philosophies on page 64 for more).

In fact, trying to time the markets can be a risky endeavour. Index fund manager Vanguard looked at the financial cost of missing the market's best days. It found that from January 2000 to June 2006, the twenty best trading days in Australia accounted for 48% of the total return. And most of those best trading days followed a really bad trading day within a month.

CHOOSING SHARES

We suggested earlier that question: 'Where will the market go from here?' is a million dollar one. Well, the question, 'Which shares will perform best?' is another one. If you don't feel you have the insight or expertise to choose shares, investing in the whole basket of listed companies via an Exchange Traded Fund or an Index Fund can be a simple low-cost option. Another is to let a professional do the share selection for you through a managed fund. The chapters 7 and 8 on managed funds and index investing have more information.

But if you want to pick and choose your own shares, here are some things to think about:

- *Get advice* – A full service stockbroker or financial planner may provide advice on which shares to buy and sell. Make sure they have an Australian Financial Services License and get a written Statement of Advice.

- *Take it all with a pinch of salt* – Understand the unreliability of forecasts. If the financial services industry really is a system of predictions and guesses about the future – which is unknown – it's very hard to know whom, if anyone, to trust.

- *Research, research, research* – Read stockbrokers' commentaries, magazines like *AFR Smart Investor* and *Money*, and the *Australian Financial Review*. Some newspapers' money and personal finance sections are good too. Consider subscribing to the Eureka Report, a website with contributions for various financial commentators and industry professionals (www.eurekareport.com.au). Read the major banks' and financial institutions' economics research papers and commentaries – they're often available for free online.

- *Don't invest in what you don't understand* – If you're building a portfolio of selected shares, make sure you understand the companies you're investing in.

- *Blue chips* – Given the market turmoil and the collapse of several second tier companies, some stockbrokers recommend looking at big, well-known companies, such as those in the top 20 in terms of their market value. They're often known as 'blue chips', though that term simply refers to their size, not their future earnings or share price growth.

If regular investing for the long-term is the name of the game, 'dollar cost averaging' is a way to drip feed money into shares on a regular basis. One of the advantages is you'll purchase shares at various prices, so when the market is low, you'll get more shares for your money. Conversely, when markets are high, you'll buy fewer shares with the same amount of money. The idea is that you'll benefit from buying more shares when prices are low and fewer shares when prices are high. This has the effect of averaging out market prices over time.

Dollar cost averaging

- *Diversify* – One of the simplest ways to manage risk is to spread it. That's achieved by investing in a diversified basket of shares. Building up a share portfolio can be costly for the average consumer as you have to pay brokerage fees each time – a more cost-effective way to obtain a diversified portfolio of shares is through a managed fund or an Exchange Traded Fund.
- *Income or growth?* – Why are you buying shares? Is it for a regular dividend income or long-term capital growth? Be aware that different shares are suitable for these purposes.

INVESTING IN SHARES FOR INCOME

While you might consider shares primarily as a path towards capital growth, they can be a good source of regular income too. Each half year or year, companies pay dividends to their shareholders. You can check current dividends, expressed in cents per share, in newspapers. The dividend yield (a percentage which changes all the time), is the dividend (cents) divided by the share's most recent sale price.

In the low-interest environment we find ourselves in today, dividends rates, or yields, can be very attractive.

Lots of different types of companies pay reasonable dividends, but let's take, for example, the four major banks' dividend yields, including tax credits, in March 2009. We've rounded the figures down to the nearest percentage.

- ANZ: 8%
- Commonwealth: 8%
- National Australia Bank: 7%
- Westpac: 8%

So you can see that the major banks' pay good dividends – often better, in fact, than the interest rates they pay their deposit account holders. If you invested $1000 in each of those shares, you'd receive

Borrowing to invest in shares

about $300 in dividends over the next year assuming the dividend was maintained. If you put the same money ($4000) in the best deposit accounts with same banks, you'd be lucky to receive half that in interest. And you'd continue to receive the dividend payments as long as you keep the investment. If the share price rises, the dividends dished out may increase too. If the dividend (cents per share) doesn't increase as share prices rises, then the dividend yield (the dividend expressed as a percentage of the share price) would fall.

The graph on page 62 shows how overall dividend yields for all companies on the share index have been increasing since 2003. By January 2009, with share prices decimated, dividend yields were about double what they were just two years earlier.

CAN YOU BELIEVE WHAT THE EXPERTS PREDICT?

When it comes to shares, advice and tips aren't hard to find. Websites, magazines, newspapers and TV regularly feature analysts and experts giving their two cents about which shares are hot and

Average dividend yields double in two years

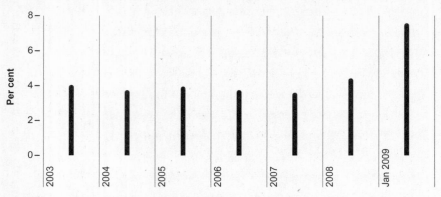

SOURCE Reserve Bank of Australia Statistics

which are not. But can you rely on these recommendations any more than you can rely on your mate's hot tip for the Melbourne Cup?

Well, talk is cheap and share tips are often wrong. Anyone trying to pick winners in their 2007 and 2008 publications had a very hard time. In 2008 the share index lost about 40% and some companies lost anywhere from 80% to 90% or more of their value. In previous years, tipping winners was fairly easy. But that's the thing about share tips; when markets are rising, as happened in Australia between 2003 and 2007, everyone's an expert and 'picking winners' isn't so difficult. When global events that the tipster hadn't thought about – such as the collapse of worthless collateralised debt obligations – cause all shares to decline, the expert doesn't look so clever.

In 2008, most of the professionals were unsuccessful investors with the majority of managed funds, super funds and share portfolios plummeting; the only question was by how much. Some of the country's top economists from our biggest financial institutions, when surveyed by the *Australian Financial Review* in late 2007, predicted that the ASX 200 would finish 2008 at between 6000 and 7000 points. The market finished the year at 3600, 40–50% lower than the experts' predictions. Similarly, in the January 2008 edition of *AFR Smart Investor magazine*, a panel of five experts predicted the year would finish between 6800 and 7500 points. Even the brightest and best get it wrong and nobody anticipated the depth that markets would crash to in 2008.

For what it's worth, investment bankers and analysts interviewed by the *Australian Financial Review* in early 2009 predicted an average increase of 27% in the S&P / ASX 200 in 2009. That increase was achieved between March and June. Many experts we spoke to predicted further stock market volatility for 2009. Nevertheless, most remained optimistic about the long-term prospects for the Australian share index.

TAX AND DIVIDENDS

Companies usually pay dividends to their shareholders from their after-tax profits. Because tax has already been paid, such dividends come with a tax credit. When dividends are declared 'fully franked', this means the whole dividend carries a tax credit (meaning tax has already been paid by the company at its company tax rate). Depending on your marginal tax rate, this means you may not be liable for any additional income tax on your dividends:

- If your marginal tax rate is higher than the company tax rate at which tax credits were calculated, you will have to pay additional tax calculated at the difference between your marginal rate and the company's tax rate.
- If your marginal tax rate is lower than the company tax rate, use the difference (the tax credit) to offset other income tax you'd have to pay (for example, on other investments or earnings).

The upshot of all of this is that for most investors, the tax they pay on dividends is less than the income tax they'd pay for other types of income investments, such as term deposits. In other words, their tax treatment can give shares an advantage over other investment options.

Warren Buffett's philosophies

Warren Buffett is regarded as one of the world's stock market investing gurus. His favourite holding period for an investment is 'forever'. His investment style includes:

- concentrating investments in world-class companies that have strong management
- limiting your investments to companies you really understand
- limiting your portfolio to about five to ten companies.

Some of Buffett's philosophies are contrary and in defiance of conventional wisdom. For example, much has been written about his belief that 'over–diversifying' your money among many companies increases your risk, which puts a twist on the conventional view that diversification reduces risk. There have been lots of books written about Buffett and his investment approaches. Check out the share investing section in your local library for more information.

Fully franked dividends

If a dividend is declared *fully franked*, this means it comes with a full tax credit (so tax has already been paid at the company's applicable tax rate). Share tables in newspapers represent fully franked dividends with an *f* beside the dividend cents per share.

INTERNATIONAL MARKETS

It's easy to become preoccupied with the Australian share market – it's what we hear about in the daily news and market reports. However, our market represents just 2% of the world economy, so it would be a little narrow-minded not to consider investing in overseas markets too. Yet 60% of the average 'balanced' investment strategy in Australia is in domestic shares, according to Barclays Global Investors.

International shares have had a topsy turvy time over the last few decades. Between 1994 and the end of 2000, the MSCI, an index of international share funds, outperformed the Australian share index. But from January 2001 to January 2008, the MSCI Index had little growth; Australian shares performed much better during that period.

Of course, there are pros and cons of investing further afield. Here are some of them:

Benefits

- *Diversification* – By looking to invest some of your money outside Australia, you're spreading your risk.
- *You can take advantage of future growth* in established and emerging international markets.
- *You can manage exchange rate risk* – Investing in overseas markets can go some way to insuring yourself against falls in the value of the Australian dollar against foreign currencies.

Risks/downsides:

- *You probably know less about international markets*, economies and companies, than you do about those closer to home.
- *The dividends you receive from international shares* won't be fully franked, so you may have to pay income tax on this income at your marginal rate
- *Some international markets can be volatile and risky.* For example, so-called emerging markets in places like Africa, Asia, Latin America and the Middle East may be more volatile than well-established markets.
- *Brokers' fees are higher for international trades*, compared to the $20–30 fee per Australian share trade that you can pay with some discount brokers.

CHOOSING A STOCKBROKER

You'll need to go through a broker to buy and sell shares. There are plenty to choose from – the first rule is to make sure the stockbroker has an Australian Financial Services Licence (AFSL), or is an Authorised Representative of an AFSL holder. Then read their Financial Services Guide, understand what services they offer and whether they suit you, and check the fees.

Basically, there are two types of brokers: discount brokers and full service brokers.

Trades only, no advice

If you just want a broker to execute your buy and sell orders (usually via the Internet), a discount broker could be for you. Trades are much cheaper than with full service brokers. The cost of individual trade usually ranges from $15–$30. Most of the major banks have a stockbroking arm – ANZ's is E*Trade and Commonwealth Bank has CommSec, for example. They let you link your trading account to your bank account, enabling you to use online banking to transfer money between accounts. Many of these stockbrokers provide daily commentary, advice and market reports, and 'buy or sell' recommendations for individual stocks. But such online discount brokers won't provide you with personal tailored recommendations or a Statement of Advice.

Full service broker

These brokers are for people who want advice about what shares to buy and sell, and a personal touch. Of course, you'll pay for this advice and service. These brokers charge higher fees (brokerage) as they provide recommendations based on in-house research. The fee for a $5000 trade is usually about 2.5%, but big trades can work out much cheaper on a percentage basis. Full service stockbrokers can analyse your investment needs, help you set goals, assess your risk profile and help you to build a portfolio that's aligned with these needs.

Big banks' online broker fees

Broker (in alphabetical order)	Product name	Trade fee ($10,000)	Inter-national shares	Analyst research	Indepen-dent research
CommSec	Internet Preferred Pricing - Website & Pro Trader 2	$19.95	Yes	Yes	Yes
E*Trade	E*TRADE Pro	$32.95		Yes	Yes
NAB OnLine Trading	NAB OnLine Trading	$29.95		Yes	Yes
Westpac Broking	Westpac Broking Integrated Accounts	$24.95		Yes	Yes

SOURCE <www.infochoice.com.au>

If you're just starting out with shares, or you don't feel you have the time or expertise to research and make share-purchasing decisions, an advisory broker could be the best option. Some brokers may not charge for this advice but it'll be reflected in higher brokerage fees each time you buy or sell shares. There's a list of discount brokers at <www.infochoice.com.au>.

For details of full service advisory brokers contact the Australian Securities Exchange <www.asx.com.au>. The ASX points out a distinction between the various brokers marketing their services; ASX 'Market Participants' (which include the brokers named in the table) are covered by the National Guarantee Fund, which can provide compensation for clients of participants in certain cases – such as when a Market Participant becomes insolvent or carries out unauthorised trades. More details at <www.segc.com.au>.

Starting to INVEST in SHARES

- *If you don't have much money to invest, you could try to start small and build your portfolio over time.*
- *Ideas for novice investors include starting with some blue chip shares, or trying an index–linked Exchange Traded Fund.*
- *Another option to start a regular share investment plan is through an index fund or managed fund.*
- *Continue to read, research and educate yourself about stock markets and shares. Get advice if you think you need it. Understand the risk of investment losses and volatility when you buy shares.*

7

Managed funds
Diversifying your investments with the help of a pro

If you don't feel you have the time, money or expertise to create a balanced investment portfolio yourself, managed funds could be the solution. In uncertain times like these, managed funds (known in the US as mutual funds) can be a great way to diversify your investments and spread your risk. But choosing a fund can be a daunting process, particularly in Australia, where there are 3432 investment trusts for general savings and investment, more than 4000 superannuation funds for accumulating retirement savings and nearly 3000 allocated pensions for income during retirement, according to investment researcher Morningstar. 'For a country with a population of just over 21 million, this gives us the greatest number of managed funds per capita in the world,' says Phillip Gray of Morningstar. 'Compare our 11 000 plus managed funds for 21 million people with the equivalent number of about 25 000 funds in the United States of America, which has nearly 15 times our population.'

When it comes to investing, competition and choice are great, but *too* many options can cause confusion. Behavioural economics tells us that excessive choice can lead investors to make no choice at all. Further to that, lots of our managed funds are very small, with more than half of the new ones containing $10 million or less in assets, 46% containing $5 million or less and almost a quarter with $1 million or less of investors' money. It seems there are just too many funds.

This chapter cuts through the confusion to explain how managed funds work, the pros and cons, the different types and guidelines for picking a good one.

WHAT ARE MANAGED FUNDS?

Managed funds pool lots of investors' money to invest in a range of assets, such as shares, property, bonds and cash deposits. The total value of the fund is divided up into small units; when you invest, you become a unit-holder. Every unit has equal value at any particular time; the more money you invest, the more units you own.

The price of units changes on a daily basis as the value of the fund's underlying assets rise and fall. Unit prices are often quoted in newspapers and on the fund managers' websites. Most managed fund investors have seen the value of their units decline recently, as underlying investments (shares and property in particular) took a battering.

Managed funds can provide investors with capital growth or loss, when the value of their units increases or declines. They can also provide a regular income, when fund managers pay out distributions to investors (monthly, quarterly, six-monthly or annually).

Advantages of managed funds

- *Different investments* – Managed funds enable you to pool your money with others and have it invested in a wide range of assets that would otherwise be out of your reach. While the average small investor's share portfolio has less than ten companies' shares, for example, a managed share fund can hold shares from hundreds of companies. Your units in the managed fund reflect the value of all those combined investments and sectors.

- *More diversification* – 'Multi-sector' managed funds generally hold a mix of asset classes and can be highly diversified. 'Single sector' funds concentrate on one asset class, but can be highly diversified within that sector. An Australian shares fund, for example, could own shares from between 30 and 100 publicly listed companies.

- *The best funds outperform their benchmarks and rival funds* – Like the top performing shares, the best fund managers can beat the market or index for a time. The trouble is picking them – see 'How to choose a fund' for more details on page 79.

- *Risk management* – Managed funds can spread your risk. If you held a small basket of shares and just one of them got into trouble – such as happened with companies like ABC Learning, Allco and Babcock & Brown recently – your wealth would also take a major dive. Big losses are still possible with managed funds when markets go south, but an individual company's poor performance won't be felt as keenly by managed fund unit-holders compared to those who have just a handful of shares in their portfolio.

- *You can start small* – Managed funds are ideal for small investors. About $5000 is enough to get started in lots of them, but many companies take on new investors with as little as $100, if they agree to make further monthly contributions.

- *They can be cost-effective* – Managed funds can be a great way to 'drip feed' regular small amounts into growth assets such as shares. This can be particularly attractive if you're investing for the medium- or long-term – and a lot cheaper than buying small parcels of direct shares regularly, as that would incur broker fees each time. Some great low-cost funds are available, but fees vary.

- *Professional management* – Your investment decisions will be taken by a pro, which means less work, and possibly less paperwork and stress, for you. While few managed funds that primarily invested in property and shares were able to give a positive return to investors in 2008, the better ones outperformed their benchmark indices after fees. In other words, their performance was negative in 2008, though slightly better than the index. Over the medium term, returns were better.

- *A pathway to international investing* – Chapter 6 on investing in shares looked at how investing some of your money overseas is a way to diversify beyond the relatively small (in global terms) local share market. And it is also a way to diversify into other currencies. In the year to April 2009, for example, the Australian dollar fell significantly in value against the US greenback, closing about 23% lower than where it started a year earlier. But if your investments were in foreign markets, you may have benefited from this currency fluctuation.

- *Potential to grow your money faster than inflation* – Managed funds investing in growth assets such as shares and property offer you the opportunity to enable your money to grow in value and maintain your purchasing power in the face of inflation, or rising prices. That said, the global financial crisis has proved that such funds may perform very poorly too, particularly in the short-term.

Disadvantages of managed funds

- *They can be expensive* – If you want a professionally managed fund, you'll have to pay for it. There's a very wide range of fees; you could pay an annual fee of anything from 0.75% to over 3% of the value of your investments. And entry fees can be a real sting – you might have to pay several per cent from every investment as an entry fee, leaving you immediately needing to make up ground. Remember, fees are negotiable and can be rebated by financial planners and discount brokers.

- *Many underperform* – Despite their high fees, some fund managers' performances don't justify what they charge. In many cases, you would have got a better return, at a lower cost, by just investing in *all* the companies in a particular market. The chapter on 'Index investing' has more about this low-cost approach.

- *Loss of investment control* – Someone else makes the decisions for you. Of course, for many investors, that's the whole point – managed funds let you leave the decisions to someone else so that you can get on with doing what you're good at.

- *Delayed withdrawals* – Some managed funds are not as 'liquid' as other investments – bad news if you need your money in a hurry. In times of market uncertainty, such as when funds have a run of investors wanting their money back, there may be a total freeze on redemptions for a period of time. This happened recently with many mortgage funds, and some property and 'fund of fund' hedge funds.

- *Some funds go bust* – A range of risky unlisted mortgage funds and debentures that hadn't been assessed by a credit rating agency have gone under, losing hundreds of millions of dollars of investors' money. Highly rated funds from large reputable financial institutions are less likely to go to the wall, however, that's still a possibility.

TYPES OF FUND

Managed funds can be used as a vehicle to put your money into just about every conceivable asset class. Research house Morningstar divides managed funds into the broad groupings of 'single sector' and 'multi-sector' funds.

Single-sector funds

These concentrate on one particular asset class or sector and can be highly diversified within that sector.

- *Share funds* invest in domestic shares, international shares, or both.
- *Fixed interest funds* invest in a range of government and company bonds.
- *Cash funds* invest in bank deposits.

- *Property funds* may invest in a range of listed property trusts (also known as real estate investment trusts, REITs), and/or unlisted property.

- *Mortgage funds* range from investment grade mortgage funds to the risky unrated types that often lend to property developers at relatively high interest rates, taking the mortgage or property as security for such loans in the case of default.

- *Index funds* invest in all or the majority of the companies in a particular index, such as the S&P / ASX 200 Australian shares index. Chapter 8 on 'Index investing' has more about this approach.

- *Hedge funds* invest a mix of assets and are supposed to profit whether markets are going up or down. They're also known as 'absolute return' funds, or 'fund of funds' because they often include a range of underlying managers. Performance has varied depending on the manager's strategy. But despite the fact that hedge funds were supposed to be uncorrelated to share market returns, many have had poor performance amid market declines.

Multi-sector funds

These funds hold a mix of defensive and growth assets. The ratio gives an indication of the fund's volatility and risk. Morningstar classifies multi-sector funds as follows:

- *Conservative funds* hold no more than 20% in growth assets, with the majority of investors' money in safer havens like cash and fixed interest.

- *Moderate funds* hold between 20% and 40% in growth assets like shares and property, and the majority in cash and fixed interest.

- *Balanced funds* hold between 40% to 60% growth assets, like shares and property.

- *Growth funds* hold between 60% to 80% growth assets.

- *Aggressive funds* hold between 80% to 100% in growth assets like domestic and international shares, and very little in more conservative assets like cash and fixed interest.

How do they perform?

The table below compares the average performance of the various categories of managed funds over the seven years to the end of March 2009. We used Morningstar's fund performance indices to illustrate how the average fund in each category fared. (Of course some funds fared much better or worse than this average.)

Most funds with investments in shares and property had a disastrous eighteen months to 31 March 2009, some declining by 30% to 50%, or even worse. Over the year to 31 March 2009, fixed interest was the star performer. Australian fixed interest funds, which usually invest in government and corporate bonds, returned 9.6% on average.

Managed fund average annualised returns to 31 March 2009

	1 year (%)	3 years (% pa)	5 years (% pa)	7 years (% pa)
Australian shares	−28.11	−6.92	5.49	4.79
International shares (unhedged)	−30.53	−14.61	−2.88	−5.23
International shares (hedged)*	−39.90	−15.48	−3.81	−3.07
Australian small companies	−37.58	−8.80	4.40	7.87
Australian listed property	−55.59	−24.85	−9.61	−3.60
International listed property	−56.06	−24.57	−4.91	NA
Australian fixed interest	9.60	5.29	5.51	5.91
International fixed interest	2.96	4.92	5.35	6.58
Australian and global fixed interest	4.42	4.24	4.86	5.69
Diversified credit	−6.44	−0.36	2.12	3.76
High yield	−10.90	−0.24	3.43	5.59
Multistrategy income	−12.14	−2.77	1.31	3.46
Multisector growth	−21.90	−6.63	2.54	2.24

SOURCE www.morningstar.com.au, April 2009. Morningstar's indices show how the average managed fund in each category performed.

* MSCI World Index Hedged to Australian dollars

NA: not applicable

Should you hedge your bets?

If you decide to invest in a managed fund that invests in bonds or shares in other countries, you may be faced with a decision about whether to neutralise or 'hedge' your exposure to changes in the exchange rate. Otherwise your investment returns would be determined by both the performance of the international shares and the Australian dollar's performance against other currencies.

The table on page 75 shows that in the year to 31 March 2009, international unhedged funds performed better (well, not as bad) as hedged funds. That's because of exchange rate changes, which favoured Australians buying shares in other currencies and then converting the money back to Australian dollars. Hedged funds declined by about 40%, while unhedged funds, which were exposed to such exchange rate movements, declined by 30%.

It's important to know that by going unhedged, you're taking two bets – one on the share market, and the other on the currency market. If the price of US shares goes up for example, but the US currency weakens against the Australian dollar, you could end up losing money. On the plus side, investing in an unhedged fund gives you some diversification away from the Australian currency. But you may decide that one bet at a time is enough.

Another option is to split your international investments, with some insulated from exchange rate changes, and others unhedged. 'Given the very unpredictable nature of currency movements there is actually a strong case for a 50/50 exposure to hedged and unhedged global equities funds,' says David Wright, Director of Zenith Investment Partners, a company that researches and rates managed funds.

However it's much better to compare returns over at least five to seven years, the minimum timeframe for most investments in 'growth' assets. Over the five years to the end of March 2009, which included both a strong bull market for about four years, as well as a huge crash, the median Australian share fund returned 5.5% per annum. Fixed interest funds on average performed about the same over this medium timeframe.

Comparing the fees

A big difference between funds is their fees and charges. This is important, because high fees can seriously detract from your long-term wealth. The less fees you pay, the more money you'll have compounding in growth over time. Some of the charges being siphoned off are very high.

Choosing the fund with the lowest fees doesn't guarantee you the best returns. But by the same token, paying high fees doesn't guarantee you good returns either. If two funds make the same investments, it follows that the one with lower fees will give you a higher net return.

Expect to pay higher fees for funds that invest primarily in growth investments like shares and property, compared to those investing in safe assets like government bonds. That's because buying and selling shares is more complicated and incurs higher transaction costs (brokerage fees). You may also pay higher fees if you go through a commission-based financial planner or adviser rather than direct, because the fees cover their commissions as well as the fund's costs.

A GUIDE TO THE MAIN FEES
CHARGED BY MANAGED FUNDS

- *Entry fee – 0–5%.* A portion of every investment you make in a managed fund may be taken as a contribution or entry fee. This means you could be down 5%, before any investments have been made; the fund will need to earn 5% before you break even (fortunately, entry fees of that magnitude aren't the norm these days). Entry fees are often passed to financial advisers as a sales or advice commission. But you don't have to pay high entry fees. They're negotiable with planners or you could invest through a discount broker that rebates commissions (see 'Where to buy a managed fund' on page 82).
- *Trap* – 'nil entry fee' funds are another way to reduce your up-front costs, but they often come with higher management and exit fees. The higher management fee in particular may erode your wealth and earnings over time.
- *Buy/sell spread (0.1% to 0.6%)* – This is the difference between the price you can buy and sell units for at any time. The buy price is always higher to discourage unit-holders from leaving the fund. So it's like an exit fee. Other exit fees may apply when you leave the fund or withdraw money.
- *Annual management fee (0.8% to 2.4%)* – The average is 1.5% and is calculated on the balance of your account and deducted by the fund manager. So if you have $10,000 in a managed fund that has a 1.5% annual fee, $150 would be deducted, leaving you with $9850. If a financial planner put you into the fund, part of this ongoing management fee may be passed to the planner as a trail commission.
- *Switching fee* – charged when you flick money between investment options (e.g. from shares to fixed interest). Some fund managers offer a limited number of free switches.
- *Performance fee:* Some funds charge up to 20% extra if the fund returns exceed performance benchmarks.

HOW TO CHOOSE A FUND

There are thousands of funds on the market, so how do you choose? It's certainly not as simple as looking at the best past performers. Get your investment goals, timeframe and risk tolerance clear in your head before you even start to compare funds.

Your investment timeframe

In the short-term, safer assets like cash and fixed interest are less volatile. In the medium and longterm, growth assets are expected to give better returns. Like all investments, managed funds can be risky, depending on what you choose. A high-growth international share fund is much more volatile than an Australian government bond fund, for example. It's critical to understand where your money is being invested and to read the Product Disclosure Statement

(PDS). Managed funds (even those investing in supposedly safe assets like fixed interest) aren't covered by the federal government's deposit guarantee scheme.

Risks and volatility

Funds with weighting towards growth assets like property and shares are more volatile than funds investing a higher proportion in cash, bonds and fixed interest. Funds in speculative investments and narrowly focused sectors can be risky. For an evaluation of the risks of various types of investments, check out the risk meters at the National Information Centre on Retirement Investments website <www.nicri.org.au>.

How much do you have to invest?

This will affect your options. Some funds require starting balances of $25000 or $50000 (wholesale funds require more), but most funds cater to small investors' needs.

Regular savings plan

Check that the fund will accept ongoing contributions and what entry fee applies. Funds often let you make ongoing payments by

Tax information

Money you make from managed funds is taxed like other savings and investments (other than super). If you receive distributions from managed funds, they should be included as income on your annual tax return. If you sell units in a managed fund at a profit, capital gains tax may apply. The capital gain should also be included in your tax return. Speak to your accountant or contact the Australian Taxation Office for more information.

Bpay (a system for paying bills over the phone and Internet), bank transfer or cheque, but minimum amounts per transaction may apply.

Compare past performance

Look at the long- medium- and short-term returns, after fees. Does the fund consistently perform well against its benchmark indices? (The benchmark for an Australian share fund might be the S&P / ASX 200 index, for example). Does the fund perform well against its peers (managed funds in a similar sector)?

However, you need to be wary of past performance. It's important to note that past performance isn't an indicator of future performance. In fact, a study by Morningstar found that the best performing funds this year are unlikely to replicate that performance in the next year (note, the study was by commissioned by Vanguard Investments, which is best known as an index fund manager). Nevertheless, Morningstar noted that the study illustrated the dangers of 'performance chasing' when investing in managed funds.

Fund rating

Check if an independent ratings company has assessed the fund. They usually rank funds from one to five stars. While the fallout from the global credit crunch illustrates that relying on investment ratings alone to choose funds can underestimate risks and lead to poor investment decisions, such analysis can still form part of your research. And if an investment fund hasn't been rated by anyone – as is common with risky debentures, unsecured notes and mortgage funds – proceed with caution. Check whether they meet the safety indictor benchmarks set by the Australian Securities and Investments Commission.

WHERE TO BUY A MANAGED FUND

When you've decided which managed fund to invest in, you have a choice about how to access it. The main options are direct from the fund manager itself, through a financial planner, or through a discount broker or website.

Direct from the fund manager

Simply go to the company's website to download the PDS, which includes an application form, or ask for one to be posted to you. Read the PDS carefully before making any decision to invest.

Buying directly can be expensive, though; the full entry fee (up to 4% or 5%) may apply to contributions. But fund managers' fees differ.

Through a financial planner

A commission-based adviser may take both an up-front and trailing commission, or one of the two, and may also charge you an adviser service fee. These fees can detract from your investment returns, so satisfy yourself that the service provided is worth these high costs. And remember, the fees are negotiable. Managed fund application forms have a section where the adviser can stipulate the fees you'll pay.

If your planner recommends you invest through a wrap account, master trust or similar investment administration service, an extra layer of fees may apply (see page 83).

Alternatively, if you need advice you could go through a fee-based planner. You'll pay a fee (in dollars) for the service they provide, just as you would with a dentist or solicitor, rather than a percentage of your investment. Make sure they agree to rebate any up-front and trail commissions to you.

If you don't have a regular savings plan outside of super, consider the pros and cons of managed funds. They enable small investors to get access to a diversified basket of assets, adding regular amounts to their fund over time. There are big differences in the quality of the thousands of managed funds on offer though – check their fees, risks, historical returns and investment policies, research agencies' opinions and read PDSs thoroughly. Don't be afraid to seek more information or answers to any questions you may have from a licensed financial adviser.

Do this TODAY

Through a discount broker

Discount brokers are mainly online financial services companies that rebate all or some of the commissions paid to them by fund managers. They won't provide you with financial advice. If you're currently in a managed fund that pays trails to a financial planner, you can switch to a discount broker and some will rebate future trail commissions to you instead.

If you know what fund you want to invest in, it's worth comparing the cost of investing directly with the fund manager itself, and through different discount brokers. There's a list of some discount brokers in Australia in chapter 11 - Getting expert advice. You should check them out and read their Financial Services Guides before committing.

Through a wrap or master trust account

If you invest through a financial planner, they are likely to recommend you set up an account with a master trust, wrap account, or similar service. They are essentially an administration platform for all your investments. Each platform might include a choice of hundreds of

8

Index investing

Index and exchange traded funds provide a simple, low-cost way to mirror the market's performance.

With stock markets having declined, you may feel that now is a good time to buy shares. If you don't know which shares or managed funds to buy, but you know you want exposure to the whole share market, index funds could be the choice for you.

Indexing is a low-cost approach to investing for the medium- to long-term. Index funds aim to track a particular market's returns – be it shares, property or fixed interest – rather than trying to beat such markets. An Australian share index fund, for example, might try to match the performance of the S&P/ASX 200 index, which includes our 200 biggest companies, before fees. An international share index fund might aim to replicate the performance of a particular overseas index, such as the US S&P 500 share market or track a combination of the world's share markets, excluding Australia.

History shows that index funds are very accurate in tracking their chosen benchmarks. In fact, the difference between the overall market's returns, and the index fund's returns, should be the fund manager's relatively low fees and the costs they incur in trading shares.

Index investing takes the opposite approach to 'active' investing, where fund managers aim to actively trade to try to beat the index or their peers. While the vast majority of the thousands of managed funds on the market are actively managed, the popularity of index funds has been steadily rising. The recent downturn has shown that many actively managed funds have under-performed the index after fees, with the worst performing Australian share funds declining by up to 50% in 2008, for example, compared to the benchmark index's 39% decline. Every year there will be active fund managers that outperform the index – the challenge for investors is finding who they are and deciding whether this outperformance can be continued in the long-term. Another option is to simply choose an index fund.

BENEFITS OF INDEX INVESTING

The principal advantage of index funds is they are cheap, so fees are unlikely to take a big chunk out of your returns (there are exceptions – see the section 'The traps' on page 87). For example, Vanguard's Australian Share Index fund, which mirrors the performance of the S&P/ASX 300 Index, charges about 0.75% per annum on small amounts, with fees reducing to 0.35% per annum for investments over $100,000. It has no entry fees if you invest directly with the fund manager or through an online discount broker.

ANZ also offers an S&P/ASX 200 share index tracker. You only need $1000 as an initial investment, and you can make ongoing deposits of $100. ANZ's annual management fee (1%) is higher than Vanguard's and its entry and exit fee is 0.25%. You need to have an eligible ANZ transaction or savings account to access this Online Investment Account.

The fund management fees are even lower if you track a benchmark though an Exchange Traded Fund, a type of index fund that's traded like a share. Their annual management fees can be as low as 0.09% (for more information on the iShares S&P 500 fund, which tracks US shares – go to the section 'Exchange Traded Funds' on page 90).

Index funds can be an easy way for small investors to start investing in a diversified basket of shares. To build up a share portfolio on your own requires a significant amount of money, otherwise broker fees will make buying individual shares uneconomical. An Australian Securities Exchange survey published in June 2009 found that the average Australian share investor owns shares in around seven companies. This exposes investors to some concentration risk – if one company goes out of business, you stand to lose a major part of your portfolio. However with an index fund, you can immediately get access to a wide range of shares with just a few thousand dollars. Like other managed funds, you can start a regular savings plan with as little as $100 per month, after depositing the initial $2500–$5000 starting balance as required.

Last but not least, index funds are tax-effective. They have a low turnover (the fund manager doesn't need to trade shares very often). This means that because they don't sell shares as often as actively managed funds, they don't 'realise' capital gains and therefore you don't have to pay as much tax.

THE TRAPS

While index investing has benefits, you need to be aware of the traps when you buy an index fund. Some of these drawbacks are:

- *You'll invest in all companies on an index.* Index investing is premised on the basis that it is extremely hard to predict which companies will do well or badly in the future so the alternative is to buy all the companies in the proportion that they are included in the index. An Australian share index fund, for example, is likely to invest in all of the S &P/ASX 200's listed companies. Inevitably, that means you'll invest in bad companies along with the good ones. It may mean you invest in companies you don't like and ones you don't think will be profitable in the long run. Of course, you'll also invest in all the good stocks that have strong growth.

- *In a downturn, index managers aren't as flexible as actively managed fund managers.* Even if index fund managers had seen the present bear market coming, they wouldn't have had the option to sell shares and shift investors' money into safe havens like cash. Index funds track their chosen market or benchmark index – in good times and in bad. However, it should also be noted, few active managers saw the crash coming and shifted money to defensive assets.

- *No diversification, in most cases, beyond a particular index or asset class.* Unlike a 'balanced' managed fund, which invests in a mix of cash, fixed interest, property and shares to spread the risk, sector-specific index funds are invested in just one asset class, such as equities or property. They're usually highly diversified *within* that sector, though, perhaps owning 200 or 300 shares, or in the case of international share and bond funds, more than 1000 securities. Diversified index funds are also available. To get diversification across asset classes you can use diversified index funds or build a portfolio of index funds.

- *They are not for the short-term – index fund managers won't outperform the index.* So in a bear market, where share prices are declining, the index fund will track the market's downward trend. Active fund managers, on the other hand, may make more prudent investments in falling markets, with some diversification into safe investments. Some commentators believe a bear market is not the time to invest in index funds.

WHERE TO BUY AN INDEX FUND

Index funds are widely available but what you'll pay, and hence the returns you'll earn, depends on the avenue you choose.

INDEX FUNDS OFFERED BY VANGUARD TO SMALL INVESTORS

- *Vanguard Index Australian Share Fund* – aims to match the total return of the S&P/ASX 300 Index before fees and expenses. Management costs are 0.75% per annum for investments up to $50000; fees reduce to 0.5% and 0.35% for larger amounts. Buy and sell spreads also apply (0.2%), as well as withdrawal fees (0.1%) to cover transaction costs. Investors can start with $5000 and make additional contributions of $100 or more via Bpay.
- *Vanguard Index International Shares Fund* – invests in around 1700 shares listed on the exchanges of 22 of the world's major economies. The management fees are 0.9% per annum for the first $50000 invested; fees reduce after that. Purchase (0.3%) and withdrawal (0.1%) fees apply. The minimum required investment is similar to Vanguard's Australian index share fund. You can choose to have the fund hedged (so your returns won't be affected by exchange rate movements) or unhedged.
- *Vanguard also offers a range of diversified index funds* that invest in a mix of assets, including cash, fixed interest, property and shares. They include conservative, balanced, growth and high growth options, depending on the ratio of income to growth assets.

Index investments from large fund managers (e.g. Barclays Global Investors, Vanguard, State Street Global Advisors) are often 'rebadged' and sold through other financial institutions.

Buy directly from the fund manager

Vanguard is the best-known index fund manager. They mak~~~ ~~~~~ ~~~
funds available direct to small investors.

Your super fund

A range of super funds offer index options as part of their investment
menu. They include personal and corporate master trusts from the
major financial institutions like ANZ, BT, Colonial First State,
MLC, Navigator and Perpetual. Some industry super funds offer
indexing options too, including HOST Plus and Sunsuper.

Through a financial adviser

If you invest through a financial planner, they may recommend
investing in index funds through a wrap account or master trust
structure. However, if the planner is paid by commission, rather than
on a fee-for-advice basis, the fees you pay for the index fund may be
higher than if you invested directly, to cover the planner's commissions.

Through a discount broker

Index funds are available through online discount brokers that may
rebate some of their commissions. The websites of several discount
brokers are listed in chapter 11 on financial advice.

EXCHANGE TRADED FUNDS

Exchange traded funds (ETFs) are *listed* index funds, which are
quoted on a stock exchange. Just like any other share, you can buy
and sell an ETF through a stockbroker or online share trading
facility. Their prices go up and down in value every day in line with
an underlying index value and are quoted in daily newspapers' share
tables. ETFs may pay dividends to shareholders.

The last decade has seen an explosion in the popularity and availability of ETFs. In 2000 there were less than 100 ETFs worldwide, and their value was under US $100 billion. Today, there's closer to 1600 ETFs worldwide and their global value is over US $700 billion.

Australians are just catching on to the benefits of ETFs. A couple of years ago, only one company (State Street Global Advisors) marketed ETFs in this country, and you could only use them to purchase domestic shares or property trusts. Since then, with the entry of *iShares* ETFs, 16 new international ETFs have been added, allowing Australian investors to buy into share markets from all over the world.

In some ways, ETFs are the financial product that many in the financial services industry don't want you to know about. They're extremely cheap – with annual expense ratios from little as 0.09% and no entry or exit fees (other than the buy/sell spread, and what you'd pay to buy and sell them through your broker or online trading account). ETFs don't pay commissions to financial advisers. That's one of the reasons that many commission-based planners don't recommend ETFs.

Why don't more planners use ETFs?

The majority of financial planners have been slow to catch on to the benefits of Exchange Traded Funds and recommend them to clients. There are a few theories put forward as to why. ETFs are low-cost and don't pay commissions to advisers, they're a fairly new product in Australia, and some advisers are slow to depart from the status quo and embrace new products. However, there are signs that this is changing. Fee-for-service and independent planners are a growing part of the advice market, and they're more likely to recommend ETFs. The benefits of low-cost investments are becoming more widely known.

managed funds, for example. That's why wraps and master trusts are sometimes known as a 'fund of funds'.

Financial planners love wraps and master trusts because they make their lives easier – for consolidated reporting at tax time, for example. But the benefits aren't always so clear-cut for investors. These 'investment platforms' can have an extra layer of fees, and do you really need to pay for the option to switch your money between hundreds of managed funds? There's more information at <www.choice.com.au/money>.

BENEFITS
OF ETFS

- *Cheap diversification* – As Barclays Global Investors puts it, you can own an 'entire index in one share'. So in a single share trade, you can buy a high degree of diversification. To build up a diversified portfolio of direct shares is out of reach for many small investors, because of the transaction (brokerage) costs.
- *Liquidity* – Some ETFs can be sold at any time with investors getting their cash within a few days. However, in other cases, ETFs such as those that are less frequently traded, are not as liquid. Do your research.
- *Transparency* – An advantage of both ETFs and index funds is that they are quite transparent. Their prices are quoted in newspapers and broad information about their shareholdings is on fund managers' websites.
- *Income* – Like with shares and funds, distributions (from underlying dividends) are paid out to ETF shareholders. Income tax will invariably apply, as not all companies in a share index pay 'franked' dividends (for more about franked dividends, go to the chapter on Shares).
- *Tax effective* – Exchange traded funds are often more tax efficient than other types of managed investments.

ETFs: what's available?

Domestic index ETFs are available from State Street Global Advisors and Vanguard Investments. They are:

- *SPDR S&P/ASX 50 Fund*– tracks the performance of the 50 biggest Australian companies. The Management Expense Ratio (MER) is 0.29%.
- *SPDR S&P/ASX 200 Fund* – tracks the 200 largest Australian companies. Its expense ratio is also 0.29%.

DISADVANTAGES
OF INDEX ETFS

Most of the disadvantages that apply to unlisted index funds will also apply to index ETFs:

- *Not diversified* – ETFs aren't diversified between asset classes, so although you'll get diversification across companies, ETFs usually concentrate on a single sector such as shares or property. So you'll have to make sure your portfolio is appropriately balanced by investing a portion of your funds elsewhere, such as in cash, fixed interest and other asset classes.
- *Foreign exchange rate risks* – International ETFs, like other overseas investments, expose you to foreign exchange rate risks. The relative strength or weakness of the Australian dollar against other currencies could affect your investment returns.
- *Not for small investors* – You need a decent sum to make each transaction worthwhile; otherwise stockbroker fees (around $30 per trade through an online broker) will make ETFs uneconomical. Small investors and those wishing to make regular modest contributions could be better off with an unlisted index fund.

- *SPDR S&P/ASX Listed Property Fund* – this fund seeks to closely track, before fees and expenses, the returns and characteristics of the S&P/ASX 200 Listed Property Trust Index. The annual management expense ratio is 0.4% per annum.
- *Vanguard Australian Shares Index ETF* – these track S&P/ASX300. The annual fee is 0.27%
- *Vanguard Total Market Share Index ETF* – these track the MSCI Broad Market Index. The annual fee is 0.09%.

- *All World Except US Share Index ETF* – this tracks the FTSE All World except US Index. The annual fee is 0.25%.

International index ETFs are available from:

- *Vanguard*
- *iShare ETFs* – are quoted on the Australian Securities Exchange and cover 16 different share markets from around the world. iShares were originally developed by Barclays Global Investors. Their management expense ratios range from 0.09% for the iShares S&P 500 ETF which tracks the performance of the large US companies index, to 0.74% per annum (for the Chinese ETFs). All ASX-listed iShares are unhedged. This means that your investment returns will be affected by the exchange rate movement of the Australian dollar against other currencies.

Superannuation – the basics

Super provides a tax shelter for retirement savings

The global financial crisis has caused superannuation's worst ever period for investment returns. As world stock markets tumbled, Australian workers saw billions of dollars wiped off the value of their retirement savings. It's quite possible that all the contributions you made to super in a whole year were cancelled out by these investment market declines. Up to three years of previous earnings were wiped out.

Such events have left many people in shock. Will I have enough money to retire? Do I have to stay in the workforce for longer than planned? Should I switch my superannuation investments from shares to cash and fixed interest to avoid further declines? These are just some of the questions nervous investors are asking.

This chapter explains why superannuation is still a good option for your retirement savings, and why your decisions about how your money is invested within super have a large bearing on your returns. We look at the basic rules, how to consolidate your accounts into one, ways to contribute more to your fund, and guidelines for the account balance you're going to need for a comfortable retirement. The next chapter takes a more detailed look at how various superannuation investments have performed, and what to consider when selecting a fund to maximise your potential earnings with an acceptable level of risk.

A LONG-TERM TAX SHELTER

While a lot of people are disappointed, worried, even angered by their fund's recent performance, the problem isn't the superannuation system itself. Super is simply a way to invest for the long term and pay less tax – but how the money is invested, and the fund you choose, is up to you. Super enables you to invest in almost all the same things that you'd invest in outside super, but you'll pay less tax on what you earn. That is, assuming the federal government doesn't change the tax laws to make super less favourable for certain investors. At the time of writing, the rules and tax treatment of superannuation is being reviewed and some changes seem likely.

Another advantage of superannuation (some would say an imposition) is that it forces you to save your money for retirement, and to live without that 9% from every pay cheque.

Do this TODAY

- *Put an evening aside to really find out about your superannuation savings. Gather all the paperwork you can first, including past statements. Find out the answers to these questions:*
- *Where is your super being invested? Do you understand the investments and are you comfortable with the strategies? Remember, this is your money.*
- *What fees are you paying?*
- *Is the fund's performance acceptable?*
- *Do you have the right level of insurance?*

Super has many restrictions too. There are limits on how much you can put in and still get the lower tax rate. You're locking away money for the long term, which generally can't be touched until you are at least 55 and retired (there are exceptions, such as early release provisions for people in serious financial difficulty or because of disability or death of a spouse).

The key point about super is it's your money and you can decide how it's invested. It doesn't have to be in the default option. It doesn't have to remain in a fund with high fees, or one that consistently underperforms against its competitors. You can take control.

What you'll pay

The big attraction of super is its lower tax. If you invested in a managed fund or term deposit outside super, for example, its growth or interest would be taxed at your marginal rate – up to 46.5%. Super isn't tax-free, but check out how it compares:

- *No superannuation entry tax applies to contributions from your after-tax salary.*
- *If you make a pre-tax contribution* – such as a salary sacrifice payment – a 15% entry tax applies.
- *The earnings or growth of your fund is taxed at 15%.* The effective rate is lower due to imputation credits and capital gains tax concessions. This tax is deducted automatically.
- *No tax applies to fund growth in the pension phase of superannuation* (when you invest the proceeds of your super in a pension to give you a regular income in retirement).
- *No tax applies to withdrawals from taxed super funds for most people aged 60 or more.* These payments are tax-free whether taken as a regular income or a lump sum. Note: Certain funds don't qualify, such as some federal and state government funds.

It's important to know that tax laws can change. These rates are current at June 2009.

PLANNING FOR A COMFORTABLE RETIREMENT

Do you know if you are on track to have enough money to retire and have a nice lifestyle? How much superannuation will you need to achieve it? The earlier you start to ask these questions, the better.

Firstly, you need to think about what your cost of living might be in retirement. Financial planners often use the guideline that after you retire you'll need 60–70% of your pre-retirement income, each year, in order to be comfortable. But a report from Westpac and Association of Superannuation Funds of Australia (ASFA), published in April 2009, goes into more detail by estimating what the average person will need for an 'adequate' and 'comfortable' standard of living after they finish working. A 'comfortable' retirement would enable you to afford being able to afford more 'luxuries', such as holidays, entertainment expenses, wine, home refurbishments and renovations, private healthcare and technology.

- For a 'modest' lifestyle, a single person retiring as at the end of 2008 would need $373 per week ($19 450 per year). A couple would require $525 per week, or $27 366 per year.
- For a 'comfortable' lifestyle, a couple would need $967 per week ($50 414 per year) while a single retiree would need $721 per week ($37 621 per year).

'The difference between the two budgets mainly relates to the extra items included in the comfortable budget,' according to ASFA. 'These include items such as being able to update the kitchen or bathroom at some stage, some wine, eating out from time to time, being able to entertain family or friends at home, private health insurance at the top rate, purchasing magazines and CDs, an economy overseas holiday and being able to afford additional alcohol or purchase tobacco or make gifts. It's not lavish – but it means the difference between a 4-year-old and an 8-year-old Corolla, and having a glass of wine a couple of times a week with dinner, rather than grape juice.'

The figures assume that the retirees own their own home. And of course, these figures are averages and individual needs vary. Cost of living is also influenced by where you live – for example, living costs other than housing are higher in country areas compared with capital cities. And what you consider to be a 'modest' or 'comfortable' lifestyle will differ from others' perceptions. However, these figures give an idea of what you'll need each year when you retire. There's more information about the retirement standard, and the estimates for the costs of particular lifestyle needs, at <http://www. superannuation.asn.au>.

Is your fund on track?

So, what size super fund would be required to provide the necessary income for retirement? Well, the good news is that according to ASFA, the government Age Pension provides most of the necessary income for a modest standard of living. But it won't completely cut it. If retiring today, you'd also need a lump sum of about $100,000 to provide you with additional retirement income required for a modest lifestyle. This assumes you'll invest the $100,000 and achieve returns of 7% per annum (and in the current environment, such returns are by no means guaranteed).

For a comfortable lifestyle, a single person retiring, at the time of writing, would need to have accumulated a lump sum of about half a million dollars. A couple would need just over half a million. The reason that the numbers are quite similar in terms of the lump sum required has a lot to do with couples getting more Age Pension than singles. While living costs are higher for a couple, the higher Age Pension makes up for this. The asset test now allows most retirees to get at least some Age Pension, including those with $500 000. As well as that, over time as people run down their capital they become entitled to higher Age Pension payments.

The estimate of capital needed for investment at the time of retirement is just one part of the picture. Again, it's assumed that the money would be invested in an income-producing investment such as a pension, and return about 7% per annum.

Reaching a 60% target

The table on page 101 shows what you'd need to contribute to your super fund, in addition to your employer's Super Guarantee payments, to achieve a retirement income of 60% of what you earned while still working. Of course, how much you'll need to top up by is dependent on how many years you have until you finish work. The calculations assume your fund has 7% annual fund growth after fees, and that your income before retirement increases by 3.75% each year.

For example, someone with fifteen years until retirement, who earns a pre-tax salary of $75 000 now ($45 000 after-tax), would need to put in an extra 35% of their income into super each year from now until retirement, to have a retirement income of 60% of the income they had while working. A younger person (with say 30 years or work ahead of them) and on the same salary would need to plough an extra 10% of their salary into super each year, to achieve the same retirement income. This shows the benefits of starting to make extra contributions early.

You need to think about the right income target for you. Some people could even aim for a retirement income equal to what they were earning before retirement – a pretty tall order. But consider what lifestyle you expect, and what it's likely to cost.

Percentage of income required above the 9% superannuation guarantee

Years to retirement	Final annual income (60% Retirement income sought)		
	$35 000 ($21 000)	$50 000 ($30 000)	$75 000 ($45 000)
10	37%	51%	59%
15	19%	29%	35%
20	10%	17%	22%
25	5%	10%	14%
30	2%	6%	10%
35	0%	3%	6%
40		1%	3%

(a) Projections based on fund net (after tax and fees) earning rate of 7% nominal and growth in average earnings of 3.75% with contributions being made by the employer and subject to 15% tax.

SOURCE Association of Superannuation Funds of Australia

TOPPING UP YOUR FUND

If the last section about the size of fund you'll need shocked you, you might want to know about the ways you can top up your fund. You may need to think about strategies to invest more in super before you retire, as well as ways to maximise your returns at the appropriate level of risk. A CHOICE report looked at the main ways:

- *Make an after-tax contribution* – You can simply lodge some money to your fund. Usually this can be done via Internet banking. No tax will be deducted from this contribution when it's paid into the fund. Tax applies to growth or earnings – see 'What you'll pay' on page 97 for more). Note that there are maximum annual contribution levels ($150 000 per annum for 2009–10), otherwise an additional penalty tax rate applies.
- *Salary sacrifice* – Making additional contributions to super from your pre-tax salary is called salary sacrificing. You need to ask your employer if they are willing to enter a salary sacrifice arrangement with you. Be aware that reducing your taxable income through

salary sacrificing may also reduce your employer's contributions to your super fund (usually equivalent to 9% of your base earnings). Try to safeguard these existing contributions before salary sacrificing, by negotiating to maintain your total package value.

- *Government co-contribution* – If you earn less than $60 342 per year (that's for the 2009/10 financial year) and make an after-tax contribution to super, the federal government will top up your fund with a further contribution. A sliding scale applies. For example, if you earn less than $30 342 (2009/10), the government contributes $1 for every extra dollar you put in, up to a maximum annual government co-contribution of $1000. In that example, you'd need to contribute $1000 to get that maximum co-contribution. The co-contribution decreases on a sliding scale for people earning more than $30 342, eventually phasing out when your income is over $60 342. The co-contribution is expected to increase in future years.

- *Spouse contribution tax offset* – If your spouse has a low income ($13 800 or less), or no income at all, you could pay money into super on their behalf. Tax offsets can be claimed – 18%, up to a contribution limit of $3000 (so the maximum tax offset is $540).

- *Pay lower fees* – Like taxes, entry fees and management fees can reduce the money working for you in super. In the worst cases, some funds charge an entry fee of up to 4% to every contribution you make. So if you whack an extra $10 000 to your fund from your post-tax earnings, $400 is immediately creamed off, leaving you with $9600. Your fund then needs to increase in value by more than 4% before you'll break even! And usually, that 4% fee is being paid to a financial adviser as commission. High management fees (1.3% of your fund's balance each year, on average) further detract from your earnings. Check out chapter 10 about making a super choice and how to find a fund with lower fees that doesn't pay fees to financial planners.

- *Work for longer, retire later* – Realistically, super fund declines of 20% and more in one year are leaving a lot of people that were close to retirement needing to extend their working lives, giving them the opportunity to contribute more to super, as well as giving the markets more time to recover.

- *Transition to retirement pensions* – When you reach 55, a Transition to Retirement Pension could help you move to part-time work before you fully retire, allowing you early access to your super benefits to supplement your income. You could continue to contribute to super through salary sacrificing. Ideally you'd still have more going into super than you're withdrawing from the pension. The pension income is tax-free after you reach 60 but tax applies before then. Transition to retirement pensions can be a highly tax-effective strategy, so good in fact that some people in the industry think it'll be withdrawn by the government. For more information about transition to retirement arrangements, check out the Appendix at the end of this book, which has useful contacts and resources.

Extra contributions to super are sometimes treated in different ways for tax purposes. Tax applies to some components and not to others and there are contribution limits. It's all a bit detailed to go into here, but you should consider these tax issues when topping up your fund. Details are available from the Australian Taxation Office <www.ato.gov.au> and the National Information Centre on Retirement Investments <www.nicri.org.au>.

DO YOU HAVE A CHOICE OF FUND?

The majority of Australians can choose which super fund to invest in. However, a sizeable portion of the working population doesn't have a choice, including *some* people who are employed:

- in public sector defined benefit funds
- under an Australian Workplace Agreement or under some collective agreements

If you're interested in switching, ask your employer if you qualify for choice of fund. If you're part of a defined benefit super scheme, be very careful about switching away from it even if you can. Get professional advice first.

How to change funds

Assuming you've decided, after research and possibly advice, that you want to switch super funds, you'll need to complete something called a Standard Choice Form (SCF). Your employer might have a SCF, or you can print it from the Tax Office website <www.ato. gov.au>. Once you've provided a completed SCF to your employer, it has two months to start directing your compulsory Super Guarantee (9%) payments to your new fund.

One of the great things about super choice is that if you change employer, you generally can bring your super fund with you. You won't necessarily have to start contributing to your new employer's default fund.

How to switch investment options

Most super funds offer a range of investment options. You could choose to direct your savings into one option (for example, the balanced or Australian shares option), or spread it between several of the options (cash, fixed interest, property or shares). Usually, the fund manager can diversify your investments for you. Most super funds offer a 'balanced' investment option as the default, for example, which spreads your money between the various asset classes.

However, the majority of super members do not make a choice about where their money is invested, with many in their employer's default fund. If that's where your money is being directed to, you should check it's suitable for your needs. You might be in a fund that's underperforming or charging you high fees, or one that's not suitable for long-term investors.

The next chapter looks at ways to diversify your investments to suit your needs, as well as analysing how the various asset classes and fund managers have performed over the last five years.

CONSOLIDATE YOUR ACCOUNTS

Super accounts often become 'inactive' when people change job or move address. If no employer contributions are going in, after a time, the money is often transferred to an Eligible Rollover Fund. These accounts can have high fees and low returns which eat away at your retirement nest egg, though there are exceptions. There's literally billions of dollars in these holding funds.

Lost and multiple super accounts have become a huge problem. There are about 30 million accounts in Australia; about 13 million are superfluous and inactive. And for investors, having multiple accounts means paying multiple fees. As a nation, CHOICE estimates that we're wasting more than a billion dollars on fees for accounts we don't want or need, and in some cases, accounts we don't even know we have.

Tracking down your inactive accounts and consolidating all your super money into one place will save you a lot of money in the long run. And who knows, your search for lost treasure might mean you'll find money you didn't know you had. Tracking down and consolidating your lost super can be a hassle and involve paperwork, but it's worth it.

How to locate and consolidate lost super

The most direct way to track down your inactive accounts is by contacting the funds themselves, if you know them. Call the contact number on your last member statement. You could also track down the name of old super funds by asking previous employers which default fund they use for employees.

If you don't have the details (name of fund, account number) of accounts opened for you in the past, have your Tax File Number handy and go to <www.ato.gov.au>. There you can search the Lost Members Register. It lists the details of about 6.4 million lost accounts, which are worth nearly $13 billion. You can also call the Tax Office on 13 28 65 to access its SuperSeeker service.

If the ATO search doesn't yield any results, try <www.unclaimed super.com.au>. It's run by the not-for-profit industry fund group Ausfund, an Eligible Rollover Fund where a lot of unclaimed or inactive super accounts get transferred when their owners can't be found.

When you locate the fund and your lost account details, the final step is to transfer the money to your active account. Your main super fund can provide rollover forms, which you'll need to complete, to prove your identity to the managers of the inactive funds, and to request the money be transferred.

Warning: some companies charge a fee to locate your lost super for you. But you don't have to pay; chances are they'll just check the same databases that you can search for free.

Do this TODAY

Make sure your super fund has your Tax File Number. Otherwise you could be paying more tax than you need to on contributions – a rate of 46.5%. Just call the fund, or check a recent statement, to see if your TFN has been provided.

Superannuation – making your choice

The choice of which fund and assets to invest in is yours but it can be bewildering.

Superannuation is the way most of us save for our retirement, but how much do you know about the fund you're in? Apart from being aware that 9% of each fortnightly pay cheque is going to super, many people just aren't engaged with how their money is being invested. And being in a poor fund or an unsuitable investment option can be a costly mistake. High fees and poor performance could leave you tens of thousands of dollars worse off than if you put some time into finding a more appropriate fund.

There are massive differences between the best and worst performing super funds, and even between investment options within the same fund. For example, in the five years to the end of March 2009, the best workplace default fund had an average annual return of over 7%; the worst lost money. In specific sectors, the differences were even more dramatic. Over five years, the best Australian share investment options with super funds provided investors with close to a 10% annual return; the worst lost investors over 3% of their money on an annualised basis. The difference between the best and worst property investment options within super was similarly dramatic.

So what does all this mean for the average worker? Well, now's as good a time as any to give your super fund a health check to see how it compares with others. If you're paying high fees for an under-performing fund, or if you're in an unsuitable investment option, it could be time to switch. Just make sure you give the decision careful consideration.

CHOOSING A FUND OR SWITCH-ING FROM AN EXISTING ONE

Listed below are some of the main things to consider when comparing funds with a view of moving from one to another.

- *Past performance* – Ads for investments have to state that past performance is not an indication of future performance – because that's true. However, it is still recommended that you check how your super fund has performed relative to its peers. If it's underperforming, you need to find out why, to see if you can change to an option that will give you better returns. The section 'How the sectors performed' on pages 116 to 117 has more.

- *Investment options* – Good super funds offer several investment options to choose from. For example, you should be able to spread your money between cash, fixed interest, balanced and growth options, from both Australia and overseas. Some investors may prefer to take more control of their super by investing it in particular shares – many large funds offer the ability to buy shares within ASX 200 listed companies. Be aware, though, that having a really wide choice of investments options can cost you in higher fees. The best super fund isn't necessarily the one with the most options to choose from.

- *Fees and charges* – Super fund fees can have a big effect on your investment returns. They include account fees, entry fees, ongoing management fees, exit fees and in some cases, adviser service fees. The Product Disclosure Statement (PDS) for each fund has a summary table of the fees and their impact on an account of a given size.

- *For-profit or not-for-profit?* – There are differences for-profit and not-for-profit funds and it's worth understanding what those are before you make a decision (see the section 'Not-for-profit or retail funds?' on pages 118 to 121 for more about this).

- *Are you in a defined benefit plan?* – Be very wary of switching out of a super fund that pays you a defined benefit (it's not dependent on stock market performance). In many cases, leaving a defined benefit fund is a bad idea. However, the risk with defined benefit plans is that they're only as strong as their parent company. If the employer goes bust, employees' defined benefit superannuation payments could be under threat too.

- *Features and service* – Does the fund offer Internet access, enabling you to check your balance, switch investment options and update your personal details?

- *Insurance* – Super funds can be a relatively cheap source of life, disability and income protection insurance. Bear this in mind when comparing funds. If you're thinking about giving your existing fund the flick, factor any insurance benefits you may lose into your decision. If you switch funds you may lose insurance cover for any pre-existing medical conditions.

- *Financial advice* – Advice is offered by almost all super funds, including most industry funds. Before choosing a fund, you may like to compare the advice services offered, the price you'll pay for that advice, and the method of payment (fee for service or commissions).

- *Retirement products* – Check whether your fund offers a pension product for when you retire, with similar investment options to the super fund.

- *Read disclosure statements* – Before you switch, make sure you read the new fund's Product Disclosure Statement (PDS). It should tell you everything you need to know. You could also consider getting advice from a licensed financial planner. And ask your employer what advice it received when choosing the default super fund for its employees. It may be able to provide you with an adviser's written report or statement of advice.

WHAT ABOUT A 'DIY' OPTION?

The number of self-managed super funds (SMSF), or 'DIY' funds, has grown exponentially in the last decade. According to statistics released in 2009 by the Australian Prudential Regulation Authority, there are now over 400 000 DIY funds and they hold about 30% of all superannuation dollars. In fact, SMSFs' market share is now even bigger than that of retail funds (28%) and industry funds (17%).

If you're thinking about joining the hundreds of thousands of Australians who manage their own super, there are some important things to consider. An SMSF is usually only worth your while if you have at least $200 000 to invest; the median DIY fund costs about $2000 per year to run and some funds cost more. To successfully run a DIY fund, you'll need to have some investment expertise and an understanding and appreciation of the responsibilities of being a trustee. You'll also need plenty of time on your hands – to take care of paperwork, write up the investment strategy, make your investment and comply with the auditing and tax requirements. You could of course pay someone to do all this – but that would beg the question, why set up the SMSF in the first place?

The huge popularity of DIY super suggests that lots of people meet these requirements. However, 2008 statistics from the Minister for Superannuation and the Australian Taxation Office throw doubt over whether SMSFs are the best option for many people:

- *DIY funds are costly and can be expensive to run* – particularly for those with small balances. High costs detract from your investment returns. The Tax Office found that 10% of DIY funds had balances under $50 000, and that was before the global financial crisis decimated super savings. If your superannuation balance is small, you might be better off joining a professionally managed fund. Ordinary professionally managed super funds with low fees might work out as better value, and some give you the ability for you to control your own money – for example, through different investment options and even share trading. In comparison, SMSFs with balances between $50 000 and $200 000 cost 2.63% to 3.55%, and SMSFs worth more than $200 000 had average costs of around 2.3%.
- *Many are too small* – 30% of SMSFs have less than $200 000. However, the *average* balance per member is over $400 000, so plenty of wealthy people have DIY funds too.
- *The trustees lack expertise* – An ATO survey found that 21% of SMSF trustees had a 'low' or 'low-to-medium' understanding of their legal obligations in running the fund. 15% didn't have an investment strategy, and 25% were unaware of the restrictions on the type of assets that could be bought from 'related parties' such as friends and business associates.

Do plenty of research before going the DIY route, free guides are available at <www.ato.gov.au>. Be wary of advisers and accountants that encourage you to open an SMSF if you don't have a lot of money or expertise – the accountant could be charging high fees.

INVESTMENT OPTIONS

Most super funds offer you a choice about where your money is invested. You can direct your money to one option, or spread it between several, adjusting your 'asset allocation' to suit your needs. Your decision – or lack of decision – could have a big impact on

> ## Warning: not always good to switch
>
> Don't overreact to short-term market fluctuations, especially if you're a long-term investor, like most superannuation members. Switching investment options can lead to better returns if you think you can time the markets, but for many people, 'staying the course' with a diversified investment strategy is a better long-term plan. If you are considering switching super fund, check what insurance benefits you'll lose (or gain).

how your account balance grows. The main types of options usually offered are discussed below.

Default option

The default option in super is simply whichever investment option the trustee selects for members that don't make an active choice – typically it is either the balanced or the growth fund. Research has shown that many people don't make a choice about where to invest their super, just going with whatever the default is for the fund they're in. Each super fund's default option is different, so performance can vary widely too. The Investment and Financial Services Association, which mainly represents super funds owned by large banks, fund managers and insurance companies, claims a lack of decision making is more of a problem for the rival not-for-profit industry funds, due to a lower level of member engagement.

Balanced funds

Balanced funds are diversified between a range of asset classes, usually with 55% to 75% in growth assets. The rest is in more conservative investments, though the genuine safety of such assets varies between funds.

Growth funds

These funds invest in a range of property and shares, both Australian and international. They'll hold a smaller proportion of 'capital stable' assets like cash and fixed interest (typically less than 25%). Growth (or 'high growth') funds are for long-term investors who are prepared to take risks and see the value of their superannuation go up and down dramatically in the short- and medium-term.

Capital stable

These funds are diversified into a range of asset classes, including cash, fixed interest, property and shares. But typically, they hold less than 55% in growth assets.

Australian shares

These funds just invest in Aussie equities, usually aiming to outperform a domestic share index such as the ASX 200 or the All Ordinaries.

International shares

These funds invest in a wide range of listed shares from overseas markets. That can include more volatile emerging markets. The aim is to try to outperform an international share index, such as the MSCI World All Countries, over the medium- to long-term. If 'currency hedging' is used, the risk of exchange rate changes is minimised (but this comes at a cost). On the other hand, if the fund doesn't use currency hedging, the investment is fully exposed to foreign exchange movements (which could work in your favour or against you, depending on how the Aussie dollar fares against other currencies).

Property

These funds invest in a variety of property trusts and funds, which may be publicly listed on the ASX and other stock exchanges (Real Estate Investment Trusts), or which may be unlisted property investments.

'Responsible investment' helps people to invest in line with their values and their financial needs. Most large super funds offer an 'ethical', 'responsible' or 'sustainable' investment option, investing in companies that perform well on these criteria. You don't have to put all your eggs in one basket though — super funds often let you divide your investments among several options (for example, their 'responsible' and 'Australian share' funds).

Some responsible funds have performed relatively well in the context of the declining markets. Australian Ethical's 'Balanced' fund, for example, lost ground in 2008, but not by as much as the Australian share index. It puts this down to its ethical investment charter, which sees the fund investing less in areas like banking and resources (such as uranium and coal) and more in sectors such as healthcare.

It's important to do your own research when comparing funds, as each ethical or sustainable fund differs in its approach and in the investments it holds.

You can check funds' research and investment methodologies at the Responsible Investment Association Australasia's website, <www.responsibleinvestment.org>.

Australian fixed interest

These usually invests in a range of low-risk assets such as government bonds. Check where your money is being invested though as managers differ. Government bonds are much safer than the bonds and debentures issued by smaller companies.

International fixed interest

These funds invest in overseas government and company bonds.

FIXED INTEREST ISN'T ALWAYS 'SAFE'

David withdrew his money from his super fund's 'cash/ fixed interest' option when he realised it was riskier than it first appeared, continuing to lose value during the economic downturn. 'I later found out why it was losing money,' David says. 'This "cash" fund actually contains investments in shares on the stock exchange which explained why a "cash" investment could lose value even when interest rates were rising.'

In fact, terms like 'balanced', 'aggressive', 'safe', 'defensive' and fixed interest' aren't used consistently across the industry, so you'll need to check your fund's product disclosure statement for its definition and for information about where it invests. For example, depending on the fund, a 'balanced' option may include anything from 55% to 75% or more in growth assets like shares and property. That's a big range. And labels like 'cash enhanced' and 'capital stable' aren't defined in law either – the median capital stable super fund lost 7% in the year to 31 March 2009 – not the solid return some investors may have expected.

Cash

They usually invests in the short-term money market and bonds, for a low, but stable, return. However there are some exceptions; sometimes a supposedly safe cash fund may invest in assets that are more volatile and uncertain than bank deposits.

Share trading

Close to 100 super funds enable members to buy and sell shares within given limits. Usually, they offer the ability to purchase shares listed on the ASX 100, ASX 200 or ASX 300 Index.

HOW THE SECTORS PERFORMED

The table on page 117 shows how the average super funds in each invest-ment category performed in the five years to the end of March 2009. The data was compiled by Rainmaker Information, which created indices which can be used as benchmarks against which you can compare your own fund's performance. The figures quoted are after percentage-based fees, but in the case of some industry funds, the member account fees weren't deducted.

Over five years, default options (where the fund invests your money if you don't make an active choice) returned 3.6% per annum. Balanced funds returned 2.6% on an annualised basis. Balanced funds invest in a mix of asset classes, including safer havens such as cash and fixed interest which offset some of the losses from shares and property.

During the same five years, the relatively stable cash and capital guaranteed sectors outperformed the other options (4.6% and 4.9% per annum respectively). Super funds investing only in Australian shares returned 4.5% per annum on average. That's due to several years of growth of around 20%, before the crash.

International shares (−2.7%) and international listed property (−2.8%) were the worst performers during the same 2004 to 2009 period.

As you might expect, over one year, 'growth' options, which invest in assets like property and shares, fared poorly. Australian and international equities (down 28%) and Australian listed property funds, which declined by 34.6%, were the worst performers over the year. Even so-called 'capital stable' funds declined in the short-term (−7%). Cash and certain fixed interest funds were the best short-term performers, giving investors respective annualised returns of 4.9% and 6.5%.

Superannuation returns to 31 March 2009

	1 year	3 years (% pa)	5 years (% pa)
Default option	–17.40	–3.80	3.60
Growth	–22.70	–6.80	2.30
Balanced	–17.80	–4.80	2.60
Capital stable	–7.10	–0.20	3.50
Capital guaranteed	3.20	4.70	4.90
Australian equities	–28.40	–7.70	4.50
International equities	–27.80	–13.60	–2.70
Property	–34.60	–11.20	–2.80
Australian fixed interest	6.50	3.80	3.90
International fixed interest	–1.30	2.10	3.10
Cash	4.90	4.80	4.60
Global fixed interest	3.20	3.20	3.90

SOURCE SelectingSuper, a Rainmaker Information company
The figures quoted are after percentage-based fees, but in the case
of some industry funds, the member account fees weren't deducted.

DECIDING ON THE RIGHT MIX

In recessionary times like these, the dilemma many people are faced with is whether to switch from shares and property to cash and fixed interest, or to weight their fund in favour of those safer options. Thoughts like these are entirely understandable, given falls in share and property markets of 30 to 50% in 2008.

If you'd shifted to cash and fixed interest in November 2007, by the end of 2008 your super fund would have been worth about 30% more than if you'd remained in the average balanced option. But you can't turn the clock back – it's all about looking forward.

Many in the industry argue that if you switch to cash and fixed interest options while share markets are at a low point, you'd effectively 'crystallise' your losses from shares. Furthermore, by switching to defensive assets, you could miss potential upswings in the share markets. Indeed, Australian shares increased by almost 25% between early March and June 2009. Chapter 6 on investing in shares has information about how costly it can be to miss the market's best days, and how difficult it is for everyone – not just amateur investors – to time the markets.

The best asset allocation depends on each individual's needs, factoring in issues like risk tolerance, timeframe and investment goals.

The mainstream way for many long-term investors to proceed is with a diversified portfolio of asset classes, which represents cash, fixed interest, shares and property, both Australian and foreign-based. This spreads your risk and diversifies among different investment markets so that you're not completely reliant on one particular asset class. Your weightings between defensive and growth assets may change over time – as you approach retirement, you may wish to lock in the gains you've made and reduce future volatility by increasing your cash and fixed interest holdings. But remember, super can remain a long-term investment even after you retire, as the money could be invested in a pension fund that provides investors with a regular income while continuing to accumulate in value for several more decades.

NOT-FOR-PROFIT OR RETAIL FUND?

Perhaps the fiercest debate in the Australian superannuation environment involves not-for-profit and for-profit funds. On one side you have corporate, government and industry funds. On the other side are retail funds, which are usually owned by institutions such as banks, insurance companies and fund managers. And while a lot of the rows are industry infighting, there's no doubt that your choice of fund could have a significant impact on your retirement nest egg.

Not-for-profits operate solely for the benefit of their members, don't pay commissions to financial advisers or planners, and have lower fees. Retail funds, on the other hand, are owned and run by financial institutions that have to provide a return to their shareholders and not just their fund members.

Retail funds' product fees are often higher than those of industry funds. Part of the reason is commissions are paid to financial planners recommending these products. Sometimes this pays for the advice that consumers receive on an initial and ongoing basis. On other occasions, the commissions pay the planners for services like processing a member's insurance claim. Some fee-for-service planners rebate the commissions they receive to their client. But in many cases, the member is getting nothing in return for the trail commissions they're paying – and for the planner it's money for jam. This case study on page 120 gives an example.

Not-for-profits, including government funds now available to the public, often finish ahead of retail funds in performance tables.

The retail funds argue that the way the returns are reported is inconsistent, because industry funds don't present fees in the same way, as the cost of advice and membership fees aren't taken away from performance figures. Furthermore, industry funds tend to invest more in unlisted property which is only re-valued every three months at best, causing a delay in accurate performance figures. A decline in the value of property could have a great impact on their value.

CASE STUDY
MONEY FOR NOTHING

Steve has two separate super funds: one has been going for 30 years, the other for about 10 years. 'They were both arranged through sales reps who receive up-front commissions and trailing commissions,' Steve says. 'One of the reps has long since passed away, and the other I haven't seen for two years. So why am I paying these commissions?'

Steve has a choice – he should call the super funds and the remaining adviser to explain that he's not receiving any service for the trailing commissions being paid. Assuming he doesn't want advice, he could switch to a discount broker and have some refunded to him. There's more about this option for reclaiming your money in chapter 11 about getting financial advice.

Making your choice

Retail and not-for-profit funds both have pros and cons. Independent comparisons of their investment returns and other details are available from the Australian Prudential Regulation Authority – go to <www.apra.gov.au> for details.

All things equal, it's better to pay low fees, as fees can drag down the performance of your fund over the long-term. If you're paying relatively high fees, which in part are funding a planner's commissions, make sure you're getting your money's worth. If you don't need their service or advice or a choice of dozens of investment options, why pay for it? You could switch to a lower-fee fund, such as a government or industry fund. Alternatively you could switch the brokerage authority to a discount broker who rebates some of the commission to you. Your super can remain with the same fund; just the third party broker/adviser changes.

*Do a health check on your fund's perform-
ance, fees and options. How do its returns
compare with other funds in its category?
Does it charge reasonable fees for the
service, performance and advice you receive?
Check where your money is invested and
whether this is aligned to your needs,
including your investment timeframe.*

**Do
this
TODAY**

Fees are just one thing to consider when comparing super funds – think about investment performance and options, who is running the fund and other factors too. To put the fee issue in perspective, in just one year (2008) of this economic downturn, super funds lost the equivalent of ten years' worth of fees due to bad investment performance, according to SelectingSuper.

Getting expert advice

In volatile times financial advice could be a prudent investment, but what are the pitfalls?

Most people wouldn't consider themselves to be financial experts, yet many of us make important financial decisions without ever consulting one. And while the financial planning industry's reputation has been tarnished by incidences of poor or conflicting advice, there's no doubt that good quality planning can help you to achieve your long-term goals.

Not everyone needs financial advice and there's no legal requirement for you to get it. However, many people can benefit from seeing an expert, particularly at life's major junctures and in times of great market volatility like at present. A planner may help you to devise a strategy to pay for a child's education, sort out your finances after a redundancy, compare the alternative ways to use an inheritance or figure out the best way to provide you with an income in retirement. Perhaps you really have no idea what to do with your money and need an overall strategic plan, covering how much to invest, what portion of your income to plough into your mortgage, and what life insurance to buy. Maybe you need very specific advice: about tax; which shares to invest in; or what super fund to choose.

Whatever your needs, experts are available. A survey by industry publication *Money Management* found that the biggest 100 financial planning groups have over 16 000 financial advisers working for them. So there's no shortage of choice. But how do you go about finding one and avoiding the pitfalls of bad advice?

WHAT ADVICE DO YOU NEED?

Firstly, think about the type of advice you require. For example, you might want a stockbroker's view about specific shares, or an assessment of the quality of a managed fund. In those cases, you'd need to understand what type of advice the planner is permitted and competent to provide. Their 'Financial Services Guide' describes what products the planner can advise on and any license restrictions that apply.

Financial product advice, which involves a recommendation or opinion about a financial product, falls into two main categories: general and personal.

General advice doesn't take your personal circumstances into account. You might contact a bank or insurance company's call centre, for example, and the person at the other end of the line will give you a 'general advice warning', so that everyone's clear that your full financial situation and objectives won't be considered. General advice can be useful, quick and often free information that helps you to understand the features of an insurance policy or savings account, for example.

'Personal' financial advice must take your needs and objectives into account. The advice should be provided in writing, in a Statement of Advice.

The laws around financial planning advice only apply to advice concerning – you guessed it – financial products. That includes things like shares, bank accounts, managed funds, super and insurance – but importantly, it doesn't apply to non-financial investments like property or credit (home loans, margin loans, and so on). So advice provided by mortgage brokers and real estate agents isn't regulated in the same way. They don't have to provide you with a written Statement of Advice. Their recommendations may be swayed by commission and other payments and incentives, but they do not have to disclose these conflicts of interest.

Members of the Financial Planning Association (FPA) however, are required by the industry body's rules to provide 'any significant financial planning recommendation in writing' – this requirement is not confined to financial products.

While licensed financial planners should have reasonable grounds for their recommendations, basing their advice on your needs, they have no legal obligation to find you the cheapest investment or insurance options.

FINDING A FINANCIAL PLANNER

After deciding what type of advice and professional help you need, start to shop around and compare planners' services. The Financial Planning Association <www.fpa.asn.au> can provide contact details for advisers in your area.

It's critical to check that the planner has an Australian Financial Services Licence (AFSL), or that they're an Authorised Representative of a licence holder. The Australian Securities and Investments Commission licenses planners, publishing details at <www.asic.gov.au>.

Financial planners generally can't provide tax advice unless they're also registered as a tax agent. Depending on how much time you have to prepare your tax return, and the complexity of your finances, making an appointment with a tax agent can be a good investment. They can make sure you get all the tax deductions you're entitled to and take care of some of the paperwork. Otherwise contact the Australian Taxation Office to do your own return for free.

See a registered tax agent

Employees or directors of a licensed financial planning company don't require individual licences – they're covered by their employer's AFSL. It's worth calling the company just to make sure the individual planner is actually employed by the business.

The planning company's Financial Services Guide (FSG) gives an overview of the license holder's business, the services provided, fees charged and commissions received. Any business relationships the planner has should also be disclosed – for example, many planning businesses are owned by large financial institutions and fund managers. They may recommend those institutions' products to clients. The disclosure of such relationships may help you to understand limitations or influences that might impact on the planner's advice.

You should find the FSG on the planner's website, and it's the first document you should receive if you arrange a meeting – read it from front cover to back. If it's not all clear, ask the planner to explain the confusing bits to you.

How will you pay for advice?

Apart from differences in the type of financial products they can advise on, a key distinguishing feature of financial planners is how they're paid. There are a range of ways – fee-for-service, commissions or a percentage of your 'funds under advice' being some of the main ones. The method of remuneration is not only important because it affects how much you'll pay, but because it can also influence the quality of advice you receive, and the specific strategies and products that different advisers recommend.

Commission-based advisers

The vast majority of financial planners in Australia are paid through commissions from the investments they recommend. Legally, they can't call their services independent or unbiased. These planners, or their financial planning dealing groups, are often owned by large financial institutions, such as banks, fund managers and insurance companies. That's not to say they can't give good advice. But past 'shadow shopping' studies of the financial advice industry by the Australian Securities and Investments Commission and CHOICE have found that in general, there's a higher risk of inappropriate advice where either the adviser receives commission-based pay or recommends products from an associated company. Planners have to 'manage' and disclose their conflicts of interest, but just because they tell you about a conflict of interest doesn't mean they don't have one.

At the time of writing, there's discussion in the industry about a move away from commissions as the standard payment method for financial advice. But even if this change goes through, it's unlikely to take full effect until at least 2012.

So for now we're stuck with commission-based advice as the standard model. But what does it cost? Usually, you won't pay a fee directly to the financial planner, but it will be deducted from your investments instead.

- *Up-front commission* – when you invest in a managed fund or super fund that the planner arranges, for example, 2% to 4% of each contribution you make to the fund may be charged by the fund manager as an entry fee. Many investors don't realise that this is often passed in full to the financial planner as their commission for introducing you to the fund. Remember, such fees aren't a one-off cost to you – they're deducted from each and every contribution you make, reducing your long-term returns.

- *'Trail' commission* – the planner is paid a portion of the annual management fee charged by the investment or super fund he recommended. This could be a percentage of your 'funds under advice', equal to between 0.6% and 1% of the value of your investments.

- *Adviser service fee* – another fee sometimes deducted from the balance of your investments by the adviser.

- *Insurance commissions* – paid to advisers are much, much higher than for investments. It's not unusual for a planner to receive a commission greater than all the premiums you pay in the first year (up to 130%), and a trail commission worth 33% of each subsequent year's premiums.

All fees and commissions are negotiable with financial planners. Most product disclosure statements have a section at the back where you or the planner can stipulate the fees and commissions to be paid.

Ask the planner to write down the fees in dollar terms, as well as the ongoing fees likely to be charged in subsequent years, and include them in your Statement of Advice.

Fee-for-service advisers

There have been some moves in the industry towards fee-for-service advice, which separates advice from product recommendations and commissions. Planners charge an hourly rate, or a pre-arranged fee for limited or full tailored advice. This can cost anything from a few hundred dollars for simple advice, to several thousand for a full financial plan.

In some cases, when a planner gives advice around super, initial and ongoing fees may be deducted from your super fund's balance.

Under the Financial Planning Association's Conflicts of Interest Principles, members should disclose their total fee for advice on both an up-front and ongoing basis, where possible.

Independent advisers

An adviser can only claim to be impartial or independent if he or she refuses, or immediately rebates, all commissions, payments and gifts received from product providers, such as investment funds and banks, to you. An adviser claiming independence also has to be free from conflicts of interest caused by links to product providers. Most financial advisers and financial planning dealer groups in Australia are affiliated or owned by large banks, fund managers and financial institutions. So they may charge you on a fee-for-service basis, but there may be a conflict of interest if they're also advising on or recommending the products of their parent company. The list of independent advisers is very small.

Recommended lists

Many financial planners are provided with lists of approved products that they're allowed to recommend to clients. They can't suggest investing in anything outside that list. If they go outside the list, their professional indemnity insurance, which can compensate consumers for bad advice, may not apply.

While recommended lists can reduce the risk that a financial planner recommends a dodgy product or one that hasn't been properly researched by the dealer group's team, one of the problems with recommended lists is that good low-cost products from companies that don't pay commissions to financial planners often aren't included. Examples include not-for-profit super funds and exchange traded funds (see page 90).

Ask about financial planners' recommended lists and understand the parameters around their advice, before signing on the dotted line.

Your first meeting

Use your first meeting with a financial planner to find out as much as you can about them. This is your main chance to find out if the adviser has the credentials, experience and expertise to provide the advice you need, and a personality that you think will lead to a good experience.

Think about the things you want to achieve by seeing the financial planner, which might include expert advice: to help achieve financial goals; to look after your dependents; a complete financial plan; ongoing advice or help with a specific problem.

Don't sign anything at your initial meeting. Use it to weigh up the planner and whether he or she suits your needs. Do the same with a few planners.

ASIC and the Financial Planning Association produced a checklist for questions to ask of planners you meet (see page 130).

Your second meeting

After deciding on a planner that meets your needs (and fills you with confidence), arrange a second appointment. You've a better chance of getting good advice if you prepare for the meeting. You will probably get more from your financial planning appointment if you bring the details of your current:

- borrowings
- dependents
- details of your will or power of attorney
- income
- insurance
- investments
- likely future expenses, such as education, housing renovations, cars and holidays
- likely health problems

CHECKLIST OF QUESTIONS TO ASK YOUR FINANCIAL PLANNER

- How long have you been giving financial advice? The longer the better. Ask if anyone else will also provide advice, such as a junior para-planner or a more senior planner.
- What type of clients do you see and what are they trying to achieve? It might be an advantage to find a planner who deals with clients who are in a similar financial position to yours.
- Do you take a special interest in any particular financial products? Are there products you don't advise on? If you're keen to get advice on super or shares, for example, you'd want to ensure the planner can help you.
- How do you go about understanding a new client? The planner should tell you that they gather detailed information about your finances and objectives.
- How do you deal with a client who has conflicting financial objectives? The planner should explain the pros and cons of various strategies, provide their recommendation and give you information for you to consider and decide on.
- What will the advice cost? The adviser should clearly explain the cost of advice, including the likely price for a Statement of Advice. Commissions received from recommended investments should be clearly explained, as well as the cost of ongoing advice and reviews in subsequent years.
- How do you keep up to date with developments? Planners should continuously upgrade their knowledge and skills.
- Are you a member of a professional association? For example, the Financial Planning Association.
- What are your qualifications? You may wish to look for a planner with a qualification, such as a degree in finance or economics. Certified Financial Planners have financial training qualifications beyond the diploma that is the minimum requirement to work in the financial advice industry.

Source of questions: ASIC/FPA

- living expenses
- risks you are willing to take
- superannuation fund
- taxes – bring your last tax return and notice of assessment.

Assessing the advice

Your Statement of Advice (SoA) is a written record of the advice that the planner provides:

- It should spell out the recommendations and the basis of the advice, including key considerations in making the recommendations.

- It should clearly indicate why the advice is suitable for your needs, and the risks of particular courses of action and investments.

- How the adviser is paid should be set out, including fees, commissions and any conflicts of interest and details of the company or individual providing the advice.

Take your time in considering the recommendations. Do they 'feel' right to you? Do you understand the strategies? Could you easily explain the recommended products to a friend? Don't be embarrassed to ask what may seem like silly or basic questions. Even major financial institutions have suffered by investing in products they didn't understand – as was demonstrated by the fallout from the global *credit crunch* and the *toxic debt* that appeared on their balance sheets.

According to ASIC, some of the issues that should be addressed or considered when preparing your advice are:

- Has the planner considered your debts, and the advantages of paying off your mortgage, car loan and credit cards, for example?

- Have the tax benefits of making extra super contributions to super been considered, as well as the downsides of locking away your money in super until retirement?

Get a fee refund

A number of licensed companies offer to rebate some of the commissions on many investments, if you switch the authority to them from your existing financial planner. It's worth talking to your present adviser before you switch. The companies, which don't provide personal advice, include:

- 2020 DIRECTINVEST <www.2020directinvest.com.au>
- InvestSMART Trail Cap <www.investsmart.com.au>
- Your Share <www.yourshare.com.au>
- iRefund <www.irefund.com.au>

These companies use different rebating models and have different costs. They generally rebate up-front commissions, keeping various portions of the trail commission. It pays to compare them. Make sure you assess their services and understand their Financial Services Guide and Product Disclosure Statement before making the switch.

- Have the risks of recommended strategies and whether they're aligned with your needs, timeframe and level of risk aversion, been taken into account?

- Does the plan recommend diversified investments? Not putting all your eggs in one basket is the first rule in Financial Planning.

- If the planner recommends switching out of your existing investments, have the pros and cons, including exit fees, been disclosed and considered?

- Has a Product Disclosure Statement (PDS) for each recommended investment product been provided and explained to you? PDSs should explain everything you need to know about an investment – often in a lot of detail. Try to read the PDS in full before investing, and if anything's unclear ask the planner or product provider for an explanation.

Heeding the warning signs

We know there are lots of cases of incomplete, conflicted or downright dangerous financial advice. We've probably all read heartbreaking stories of retirees losing their life savings and even their homes after following shonky advice or investing in risky products they didn't really understand.

An adviser's Financial Services Licence or membership of a professional association may improve the chance that you're in safe hands, but really those things are no guarantee – they're the bare minimum you should expect. It's possible that could still receive bad advice or even get ripped off. ASIC regularly bans financial advisers and cancels their licenses.

However, we can learn from past experience, and financial disasters that provide warning signs to watch for:

- *High commissions on investments* – If the adviser receives commissions that are higher than industry norms, that's a big warning sign that the investment could be risky. It could also indicate the planner is putting his interests ahead of your own. The level of commissions is usually indicated by the fees you'll pay. An investment fund entry fee above 5% should set your alarm bells ringing, for example.

- *Promising high investment returns with low risk* – Those two things are mutually exclusive.

- *Non-mainstream investments and strategies* – Be wary of investment gimmicks, get-rich-quick schemes, and investment 'secrets'. Reputable planners use tried and trusted strategies like diversification into quality investments.

- *Investing for tax breaks* – Weigh up the pros and cons of the investment itself, not just the tax advantages it receives. For example, agricultural projects, such as olive tree plantations and emu farms, are sometimes promoted as investments, with the lower tax rate on these projects their main selling point. Be wary. The promoters often receive high commissions (up to 10%) for selling these 'tax effective' investments. Such high commissions may compromise the adviser's independence and objectivity.

- *Non-financial products* – Advice around these products is generally unregulated and consumer protection is lacking. Investors have been badly burned by schemes that enable them to invest their self-managed super funds in art and wine, for example. The 'two tier' marketing of investment property is another example to be aware of – where real estate agents fly investors in to a location and inflate the property prices above what the local market would pay. It's important to recognise when advice is unbiased or conflicted.

Need a second opinion?

If you're not 100% sure about the financial diagnosis you receive, why not get a second opinion? If your physical health was at stake, you'd probably see a second doctor.

You should also do your own research into the recommendations. For example, if a particular managed fund has been suggested, you could check out whether it has been evaluated by a research house or credit ratings agency. If you're really unsure, you could pay another planning firm to review and give an opinion on your Statement of Advice. If the planner has recommended a financial strategy that you don't really understand, such as borrowing to invest in shares (a margin loan), you could read up on what independent organisations like ASIC, the National Information Centre on Retirements and CHOICE have to say about the pros and cons of such strategies (see the Appendix for some useful contacts and resources).

STEP-BY-STEP GUIDE TO
USING A FINANCIAL PLANNER

The planner must hold an Australian Financial Services Licence (AFSL), or be an Authorised Representative of a licence holder. Go to <www.fido.gov.au> or call 1300 300 630 to check. ASIC will tell you if the planner has been banned. All planners are to be part of a recognised external dispute resolution scheme for consumer complaints (the Financial Ombudsman Service, for example).

- The peak body for the industry is the Financial Planning Association (FPA). Members are required to follow a code of practice and are subject to professional accountability standards. You can find a certified Financial Planner through the FPA website at <www.fpa.asn.au>
- Check the planner's qualifications, training and experience.
- Read the planner's Financial Service Guide.
- Think about how you'd like to pay for advice. Fee-based advice is less likely to be influenced by commissions and conflicts of interest. Find out what your Statement of Advice will cost, and the cost of ongoing advice if provided.
- Ask who owns the planner's business, as this can influence the services and products offered. Check what sort of investments and products they recommend, and if the license places any restrictions. Ask what research the planner uses when recommending products. Find out if the planner specialises in particular areas that are suitable for you.
- Note there's no compensation fund for victims of bad advice.
- Negotiate fees and service. Financial planners must disclose all fees and commissions and any other incentives that could influence their advice.
- Ensure you receive a written Statement of Advice and PDS for any products that are recommended.
- Monitor your investments' performance and any fees or commissions being deducted on an ongoing basis.

IF THINGS GO WRONG

If you invest in a financial product and want to change your mind, most have at least a 14-day cooling off period. Use the couple of weeks after you start to invest to read the PDSs again, to be absolutely sure you've made a good decision.

If you're unhappy with the advice you receive, you should first approach the financial planning company and the license holder's internal dispute resolution scheme. If that doesn't resolve the issue, you can lodge an official complaint with an external dispute resolution scheme. All Financial Services Licencees are legally required to be a member of a complaints scheme approved by ASIC. Planners are members of the Financial Ombudsman Service (see Appendix for information).

Make sure you also lodge official written complaints with the financial planning company and professional associations that it's a member of. The FPA, for example, can investigate and sanction members if they breach its code of conduct. FPA members are subject to the association's Professional Accountability Measures – details at <www.fpa.asn.au>.

Free financial health checks	Occasionally, financial institutions and planners offer a free financial health check or meeting. While the meeting may help you to assess your situation and needs, it could also effectively be a teaser to encourage you to arrange further meetings, or to invest in products that the planner recommends or promotes. Some planners may say their advice is free, but remember, someone is paying for it!

12

Your castle

Australians love to invest in property, but are we paying too much?

When we buy shares or bonds, all we see is numbers changing on a computer screen. You can't touch, feel or 'kick the tyres' of these investments, and it's hard to find an 'emotional' connection. So with financial markets plunging, it's not surprising to see a renewed interest in property investment. Unlike the flickering numbers, bricks and mortar are tangible and real — you know a house you purchase will still be there in five, ten or fifty years time, while you can never be sure that shares in a company won't have gone down the tubes. And if you buy a decent property in a reasonable location, there's a good chance that there'll be demand for people to live in it or buy it.

Of course it's not just investors that are again starting to dip their toes in the real estate market; the federal government's increased grants and incentives for first-home buyers are encouraging more people to get a foot on the ladder. The Reserve Bank's slashing of interest rates is another reason lenders are seeing a surge in loan applications, as mortgages become more affordable. In some suburbs in Australia, under certain circumstances, the monthly mortgage repayments on a property are cheaper than what you'd pay a landlord to rent the same place.

However, there's an elephant in the room – the question of whether Australian property could be overvalued. We continue to chase the home ownership and property investment dream, but are we paying too much? Are government incentives and grants, which prop up the market, luring unwitting first home buyers into the trap of overvalued houses and apartments?

MEASURING AFFORDABILITY

By mid-2009 interest rate cuts, homebuyer grants and relatively stable property prices made housing the most affordable it's been in seven years, according to the Housing Industry Association. With the Commonwelath Bank, it compiles a first home affordability index that considers first home prices, median income and interest rates. But how do we compete internationally? A 2009 report by the US-based Wendell Cox Consultancy looked at housing affordability in 265 markets across Australia, Canada, Ireland, New Zealand, the United Kingdom and the United States. To measure housing affordability, the Demographia report (the 5th Annual Demographia International housing Affordability Survey: 2009) looked at the median (or middle) house price in each area, comparing it with median household income in the same market. It then calculated the 'median multiple' to assess affordability. For example, if median household income in a city was $50 000, and the median house price was $250 000, the median multiple would be 5.

The median multiple is one of several credible ways to measure affordability. Two of the key determinants of affordability are mortgage interest rates and income to house price ratios. 'The simplicity of the median multiple measure is its strength,' says Wendell Cox, one of Demographia's authors.

Demographia considers that a median multiple of 3 or under signals an affordable market, but after that affordability gets stretched:

- Median multiple of 3 or less: affordable
- 3.1 to 4: moderately unaffordable
- 4.1 to 5: seriously unaffordable
- 5.1 or higher: severely unaffordable.

The report found that in the countries compared, 28% of markets ranked as 'moderately unaffordable', 15% 'seriously unaffordable' and 24% 'severely unaffordable'. The vast majority of affordable housing markets were in the US, where house prices have fallen by about 20%. There were a few affordable housing markets in Canada. But none of the affordable markets are in Australia or the other countries.

The data collected is from the third quarter of 2008, so it would have taken into account moderate property price declines in Australia that year. It would also have incorporated a lot of the housing crashes and slumps – for example, the US house prices down by 20% and UK prices down by 12%.

AUSTRALIA 'SEVERELY UNAFFORDABLE'

The report included 27 locations in Australia and found that *none* fell into the affordable category. There weren't even any Australian markets in the 'moderately unaffordable' category. Three areas were considered 'seriously unaffordable' (Ballarat, Bendigo and Wagga Wagga). But the vast majority – 24 markets in Australia including all our major cities – were found to be 'severely unaffordable'.

The big problem, according to Demographia and others, is state and local government planning policies that ration land for development – called urban consolidation. It claims that if such policies weren't in place, there'd be no shortage of housing. While demand for housing affects prices, others here noted that on the supply side, efforts to improve housing affordability should be focused on policies regarding land use and on improving the efficiency and supply of housing.

Demographia's report stated that 'unlike the other national markets in the survey, Australia has thus far been able to avoid material house price declines. It seems likely that, sooner or later, the inherent instability and non-sustainability that characterises bubbles will lead to house price declines in Australia. However, were it possible for Australia to retain its highly over-valued house prices, there would still be a significant cost. Future generations would pay far more for housing than in the past, and Australia's relative standard of living would decline.'

'There is no house price bubble'

As you'd expect, Demographia's report and the implication that Australian property is overvalued, aren't popular in some quarters. A criticism of the Demographia report is that it only uses prices for houses, not apartments. Other affordability measures compare the median price of all dwellings with households' after-tax disposable income, suggesting fewer affordability problems in Australia (for examples, see papers and speeches at <www.rba.gov.au>). Critics say Australia's specific circumstances make our residential property market unique and certainly unlike America's. First, they say housing supply here is insufficient to meet demand, unlike the USA where there's simply too much housing. We also have urban consolidation practices (to contain urban sprawl) that prevent land planning approvals, and a rising population that will continue to need housing. Furthermore, banks'

Affordability in our major cities declines

In the early 1980s, you could buy an average house in Adelaide, Brisbane, Melbourne or Perth with about three times the average household income. Even then, affordability in Sydney was low, with the median house costing five times median household income.

However, the graph shows the dramatic change in affordability in those five capital cities, between 1981 and 2008. Even though more families have double incomes now, housing affordability is more than twice as bad compared to the early '80s. By 2008 the median house price in Sydney was $529 000 and the median household income $64 000, giving a multiple of 8.3. See the chart below.

Housing affordability in major Australian cities 1981–2008

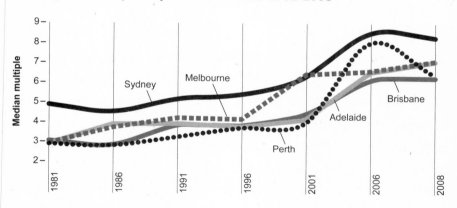

SOURCE Demographia

lending standards in Australia have been by and large much better than in the USA, with far fewer 'sub-prime' borrowers, defaulting loans and 'distressed' sales.

Tim Lawless is Research Director with RP Data, a company that analyses house and rent price changes across Australia. 'I wouldn't

How will unemployment affect house prices?

Perhaps the most significant pressure facing house prices is the threat of rising unemployment. It's all very well saying that demand for housing will continue to exceed supply, but the question is what price will people be able to pay, especially if they're out of work or not earning as much money as they could be. It's likely that as unemployment rises, we will see more borrowers defaulting on their loan repayments and being forced to sell up. The rise in unemployment in the early 1980s and 1990s led to significant falls in real (adjusted for inflation) house prices.

Tim Lawless of RP Data says that although unemployment, which was up to 5.5% by mid-2009, is widely predicted to increase to at least 7%, it hasn't yet affected property prices. 'If unemployment rises beyond 8%, we are likely to start to see the problems reflected in the property market,' Lawless says. 'At that point property prices could decline, as distressed sales increase. At present the market is relatively flat.'

agree with Demographia's findings, the measures are too simplistic,' Lawless says. 'The report doesn't take into account different housing styles – in other major cities around the world it is very rare to find detached housing within 5 or even 10 km of the city, let alone waterfront houses. Demographia's findings seem sensational, but I disagree with how they determine what's affordable and the data they use.'

Monique Wakelin, a property investment adviser and author of two property investment books, is also critical of Demographia's methodology, which she sees as one-dimensional. 'The simple comparison of income to prices is flawed and doesn't add up,' Wakelin says. 'Every national economy will be in a different position and can't be compared like this. We borrow differently in Australia compared to other countries – we have very high levels of equity in our properties, and just 35% of households have a mortgage. There is no house price bubble in Australia. We're not going to have a crash.'

That the report doesn't take account of local details does seem a reasonable criticism. Queensland's Sunshine Coast, for example, was considered to be our least affordable property market, comparing local house prices to wages. But this figure doesn't take account of the number of retirees from places like Melbourne and Sydney bringing their higher wages from their working lives to the Sunshine Coast. Demographia points out that the median house prices were far lower in the Sunshine Coast and similar places in the past; they've risen because the supply of housing hasn't been allowed to keep up with demand.

Before you get too comfy ...

There are a few outspoken people predicting a massive fall in house prices and others saying we're likely to see substantial decreases or a 'soft landing'. Some gave their vews in March 2009.

Steve Keen, Associate Professor of the University of Western Sydney, thinks Australian house prices could fall by as much as 40% over the next 10–15 years. He writes about this in the blog at <www.debtdeflation.com>. The Morgan Stanley economist Gerard Minnack also speculates about the possibility of house price declines of 20% to 30%, citing high debt levels as the main driver of our high property prices. Professor Robert Shiller of Yale University has called US housing price bubble the biggest in world history, predicting there will be further declines.

Bruce Baker, a Queensland financial planner, also says the long-term data suggests we will get a 50% crash in house prices. 'Bubbles inevitably burst, fact,' says Baker. 'And Australian house prices are in a price bubble. Australia seems likely to have a similar house price crash as the USA; that is, 50% over the next few years, caused by the same issue as in the USA – a bursting speculative bubble. This assessment is based on looking at the Australian Bureau of Statistics house price data, through the lenses of a Professor Robert Shiller analysis perspective – and unfortunately Professor Shiller's forecasts seem to becoming true. According to ABS data, Australian average house prices have doubled in real terms since the mid-1990s – similar to the experience in the USA – driven by the same factor – a growing debt bubble which is the biggest debt bubble in Australia's history. A natural conclusion is that a house price bubble created by the largest debt bubble, is likely to be followed by a historically large house price crash. This seems to condemn Australia to a somewhat similar fate as the US economy. Australia's house price crash seems to have just commenced.'

AMP Capital's Chief Economist Shane Oliver, while pointing out the factors in the Australian market's favour, says our house price bubble has been bigger than both the United States and the United Kingdom. However, AMP doesn't believe we'll have similar price falls. 'On balance we see average house prices falling another 10% to 15% over the year ahead,' says Oliver. 'Australian housing remains highly overvalued, by an average 23%. It needs to fall by about that amount to return to more normal levels. The ratio of house prices to median household income in Australia is more than double what it is in the US. But barring a very deep recession, 40% falls in house prices are unlikely.'

ANZ's Head of Property and Financial Systems Research Paul Braddick is confident that conservative lending by Australian banks will prevent a US style collapse in house prices. 'Despite rising unemployment, we continue to believe that Australian house prices will remain relatively well-supported and will not experience anything like the spectacular falls that have occurred in the US, UK and other developed countries,' Braddick says. 'Though risks remain, we believe Australian house prices will experience a relatively soft landing. We expect the median house price to fall by

What is negative gearing?

If you have an investment property and your costs in owning and maintaining are higher than the income you receive (rent from tenants), you can soften the blow by claiming this investment loss as a deduction on your tax return. This means the property is negatively geared. The idea is that although you're losing money now, you're taking a bet that the property will rise in value in the long-term to give you a profit.

The main cost that can be considered for a deduction are your mortgage interest repayments, but certain other costs are allowable too. Go to the Tax Office website <www.ato.gov.au> for details.

around 6%, which while significant, pales next to the 50%+ (and counting) collapse in equities. We currently estimate that by mid-2010 Australia will have an unprecedented housing shortage of 250 000 dwellings.'

Even if the dire predictions of a 40–50% crash in property prices turn out to be wrong (and home owners and others across Australia are hoping that's the case), the income to house price ratios serve as a warning, particularly to those entering the property market for the first time. The median multiple isn't a perfect predictor of future trends – it's not supposed to be. It's a broad indicator that shows beyond any doubt (and irrespective of the reasons) that for many of us, houses are severely unaffordable. Coupled with our big mortgages, the situation could prove very precarious for borrowers throughout this recession. Thankfully, interest rate cuts have eased the strain for many borrowers.

DOES THIS MEAN I SHOULDN'T BUY A HOUSE?

It is not that property – to live in or as an investment – is to be avoided. But it would be remiss not to point out the relative expensiveness of Australia's house prices in international terms. Some academics and experts are worried that this is not sustainable. Others don't seem so concerned. In fact, the Reserve Bank of Australia stated in 2009 its view that the Australian housing market will hold up better than countries such as the US and UK, where price falls have been in the order of 20%. But if a house price correction does happen, it shouldn't catch you completely by surprise.

There are a few sensible things that we can all do when investing in property or any other asset:

- *Research, research, research* – Speak to experts, friends, family. Visit your local library or bookshop – there are lots of good books about property investing. For the warnings and what to watch out for, check out Neil Jenman (books available widely and through <www.jenman.com.au>).

- *Save the biggest deposit you can* – to reduce what you have to borrow and the additional mortgage insurance that applies if you have less than 80% of the purchase price.

- *Don't blindly follow the belief that all property doubles in value every 7–10 years* – (According to Monique Wakelin, this can only apply to good quality properties with high yields within 5–10 kilometres of major cities.)

- *Look at the rental yield* – you'll receive for an investment property. This is a function of the price you pay for the property, and the rental income you receive, which may change.

- *Do a 'what if' analysis* – What would happen to your finances and ability to repay your loan if you couldn't find a tenant, if interest rates rose by 3–4%, if you lost your job or if property markets and rental yields generally declined?

- *Make sure you have building and contents insurance* — for your home, and landlord's insurance for your investment property.

- *History shows that property markets, like share indices, rise and fall* — It's highly debatable whether the past property market price booms can be sustained and repeated into the future.

- *Remember Investment 101 says you should diversify your investments* — If you put all your money into an investment property and find that you bought at an inflated price, the property market declines or your ability to pay the mortgage changes, you could find yourself in financial difficulty.

- *The idea that we all need to get a foot on the property ladder is a powerful one* — Think about the symbolism — ladders point upwards and if we don't get a foot on that first rung, perhaps we'll never be able to climb towards home ownership and wealth. While building up equity in your own home (instead of renting) can be a great move, the truth is that property prices, like ladders, can go in two directions — up and down.

Who can you trust?

If you're buying or selling a property, do plenty of research and get a range of opinions. Be aware that property advisers aren't licensed in the same way as financial advisers, so they don't have to give you a written statement of advice demonstrating that their recommendations are in your best interests. They do have to abide by Fair Trading legal requirements and industry bodies' code of ethics.

Whether you're buying or selling, an independent and licensed valuer is recommended, to put a real and accurate price range on the property. Different real estate agents will often give a wide range of estimations for the same property. They give 'free market appraisals', but some may give you an unrealistically high price estimate to encourage you to sign with them as your sole agent. Other agents may give low price estimates so that they can get a quick easy sale and pocket the commission.

A huge industry machine promotes Australian property as a top investment. But few of the people giving this advice can be considered unbiased and independent – they have something to gain, whether they're sellers' agents trying to sell properties to earn commissions, or developers selling apartment blocks. Expect the advertising of property investment opportunities to continue and grow as share market volatility continues. After all, property's big selling point is its perceived lack of volatility and intrinsically 'solid' nature.

There's likely to be a continued encouragement to investors to borrow to invest in property. Back in October 2005, the Senate's Economics Reference Committee reported that among the main causes of increased household debt was 'the growing acceptance of the concept of debt used for investment as 'good debt', actively promoted by financial advisers promoting wealth-creating strategies based on investment in equities and property.' Many of those who borrowed to invest in shares were burned when share prices plummeted. Property investors should also recognise that property markets aren't guaranteed to rise, particularly in the short-term.

Avoiding a personal credit crunch

Repair your personal balance sheet and use credit cards to your advantage.

During the last decade of our spending boom, it seemed like our love affair with credit cards would never end. Ten years ago, we had about eight million credit card accounts; today there's over 14 million. During the same decade, the value of both our card purchases and our credit limits jumped by over 300%. Long before the credit crunch, there was a credit boom, and while there are definite signs that it's slowing, credit card spending is now ingrained in our culture.

For many, plastic really is fantastic. Credit cards can provide an easy and convenient way to pay for just about anything. What's more, by paying with a card you can use someone else's money, have more than a month to clear the debt and pay no interest. The statistics show that overall our level of repayments increased in line with the increase in the number of accounts and transactions we made with our cards. It seems living in this plastic society is easy.

Or is it? The government statistics also confirm that over the last six years, the total card debt we're failing to repay has doubled.

We read a lot about the 'credit crunch' that gripped world financial markets and led to global recession, but there's another credit crunch happening in homes the length and breadth of Australia. The number of credit cards that are accruing interest each month is rising and by early 2009 the total amount accruing interest stood at nearly $33 billion – the average card account has unpaid debt of $2300, an increase of over 43% since 2003. While the recession has definitely caused people to change their credit card behaviour by paying off more debt and reducing their credit card purchases and cash advances, our card debt remains close to an all-time high.

It's not hard to see how we got ourselves to this point – credit card offers are everywhere, almost anyone can get one (or two, or three ...) and some of the credit limits being dished out are excessive – the average credit limit per account is around $8600. Financial institutions use psychological tricks to get us to agree to bigger limits and more spending – you may have received a letter in the mail saying something like 'congratulations, you're pre-approved!' from a card company you never applied to. Most of us know someone with a 'maxed out' card, or a credit limit far greater than they can afford. And to make the problems worse, despite the Reserve Bank's slashing of interest rates, some banks have actually raised their interest rates and profit margins on credit cards, increasing the chances that spenders will be whipped away in a spiral of debt.

Whether you're in control or feeling like your card is controlling you, this chapter provides information to:

- rein-in credit card debt and get back on track
- find a card with lower fees or interest, and more interest-free days – a good idea even if you use your card smartly
- avoid sneaky tricks and hidden charges.

The final section of this chapter investigates store credit – those 'buy now, pay later' deals – and how to dodge their traps.

TEN WAYS TO AVOID A CREDIT CRISIS

First things first – if you don't use your credit card smartly it's going to be one of the most expensive ways to borrow money. Some card sharks are charging over 20% annual interest. And it's not just the interest that you need to worry about, the big banks' fee income from credit cards increased by 170% in just five years. Meanwhile, an increasing array of sneaky tricks is being employed by the card companies, with the sole aim of making sure you part with your money.

However, making credit cards work for you is well within your control. Here are the ten golden rules:

1 *Pay your bill on time and in full* – it is the only way you can avoid a hefty interest bill. Don't just repay the minimum monthly repayment the card provider asks for (for example, 2% of your debt). If you continually just pay the monthly minimum, it'll take years (or even a lifetime) to get out of debt. One way to make sure you repay you bill in full is to activate your bank's automatic sweep facility, or pay by direct debit.

2 *Pick the best card for your spending pattern* – Credit card users can be divided into three broad categories:
   • 'Always payers' have no problem spending within their means and clearing their bill on time each month.
   • 'Occasional late payers': sometimes don't pay on time or in full.
   • 'Never payers' are known in the industry as 'revolvers'; they tend to carry card debt from month to month without repaying it.
   Be honest and determine which category you fall into, because it will greatly influence the best type of credit card for you. Then go to page 154, 'Choosing the best card' for a suitable option.

3 *Keep track of your card use* – Sometimes, whacking purchases on to the plastic somehow seems different to spending 'real money'.

Armed with a wallet full of cards, we tend to buy more things than we would if just using cash. Psychological studies have proved scientifically what we all know to be true intuitively – we spend more money when using plastic instead of cash. Keeping track of spending is enough for many to avoid it getting out of control. Register for Internet banking for easy monitoring. If you find you're spending more than you can afford, leaving the card at home or taking a pair of scissors to it could be the most sensible choice.

4 *Only spend what you can afford to repay this month* – Credit cards should make life easier, but not cause you to rack up debts at high interest. There are much cheaper ways to borrow money, so only use your card for what you're certain to repay each month. If you're struggling to contain your spending, try a self-imposed 'no credit card month' to help you get back on track.

5 *Avoid owning too many cards* – There's nothing wrong with having a couple of cards if you're disciplined. You might have one for regular use and another for the occasional overseas purchase – for example, a card with no foreign exchange fee. But if you lack discipline, several cards can be hard to control, leaving you with a pile of bills to cope with and the temptation to spend, spend, spend. Added to that, you could be paying multiple annual fees – what a waste of money!

6 *No cash advances* – One of the worst ways to waste money is to use your credit card for cash withdrawals. As soon as the ATM spits out money your interest clock starts ticking – there are no interest-free days with cash advances. Plus the interest rate is often higher than the rate for purchases, and you'll be charged a fee of around $1.50 for each withdrawal (even more when you are overseas).

7 *Reduce your credit limit* – Some of us start with limits that are simply too high; others get drawn into increases by clever marketing. Financial institutions have been accused of using psychological tricks in their marketing to encourage consumers to apply for cards they don't need and huge credit limits they can't

afford. You might think having a $7000 limit is okay because you don't have to spend it, but in reality many people are lulled into a false sense of security and rack up too much debt. Big limits can also affect your credit rating if you apply for a mortgage or a car loan. So if your limit is over the top, just call or write to your card company to get it reduced to a saner level. Be aware, though, that this won't necessarily stop overspending because cards allow you to exceed your credit limit – and then charge you hefty fees.

8 *Don't get penalised* – Penalty fees have been a bonanza for the card providers. On average, you'll be penalised by about $30 each time you pay your bill late or exceed your limit. Some banks even charge up to $40. Avoid these penalties by paying your bill on time and keeping an eye on your credit limit– don't exceed it! If you do get slugged with a penalty fee, you may be able to have it reversed. CHOICE and the Consumer Action Law Centre think such penalty fees are excessive and even unlawful – many customers have had them successfully refunded by following the tips at <www.fairfees.com.au>.

9 *Understand how your card works* – Card providers use a bewildering array of confusing methodologies to slug their customers with fees and interest. Most of these costs can be avoided if you know how your card works. Check out 'Five sneaky tricks to avoid' and take a few minutes to read the Terms and Conditions (T&Cs).

10 *Reward yourself* – Rewards schemes can enable high spenders who spend at least $2000 on their card each month to earn enough points to enjoy free flights, shopping vouchers and other benefits. However, cards with rewards can have high annual fees – $85 for a standard rewards card or $140 for a gold rewards-based card, compared to $29 or even no annual fee for a card without rewards. To get any benefit from rewards cards you'll need to spend quite a bit and always repay your monthly bill in full and on time to avoid interest. If you're an occasional late payer (see page 154), don't waste your time and money on a rewards card as you'd be better off with a low interest rate. Chasing rewards while paying big interest bills is a false economy.

CHOOSING THE BEST CARD

There are hundreds of credit cards on the market so choosing the right one can be tricky. You need to find one that suits the way you spend and make repayments.

Always payers

If you follow golden rule number one and always pay off your monthly bill in full and on time, look for a card with a low annual fee and a good number of interest-free days for purchases. As you don't pay interest, the rate isn't so important. For up-to-date rates and fees, check out the websites listed at the end of end of the book.

Never payers ('revolvers')

If you can't clear your debt and get back to interest-free days, a credit card may not be the best option for you. If you're convinced you need one, look for cards with a low interest rate and annual fee. Also consider the alternatives – such as a debit card which allows you to withdraw straight from your bank account, or consolidating your debt to a lower interest rate a personal loan or a card that offers 0% on balance transfers. For more tips for never payers, see the section 'Getting back on track' on page 155.

Occasional late payers

If you occasionally miss repayments and don't pay your bill in full by the due date, apart from making sure your interest rate and annual fee are competitive, choose a company that calculates your interest fairly. CHOICE found that at least ten different methodologies are used, some fair and others downright punitive. Bendigo Bank and NSW Teachers Credit Union are examples of 'fair' interest chargers. If you don't pay your bill in full by the due date, those institutions use one or more of the following methods to calculate interest:

- interest applies only to amounts that are unpaid by their due date – you get rewarded for partial repayments
- interest is charged only from the date the new statement was produced, not all the way back to when original purchases were made.
- an interest-free or 'grace' period applies for new purchases even if you're carrying an unpaid debt from the previous month.

Less generous card companies use a variety of tactics to extract the maximum interest from people who don't always pay in full or on time.

GETTING BACK ON TRACK

If you're carrying card debt, getting that under control should be a top priority. That just means paying off your card and limiting its use to what you will definitely be able to repay on time. But be honest with yourself – if you simply can't afford to clear the debt you should consider the alternatives for getting out of trouble:

- *0% for balance transfer*s – Consider transferring your debt to a card that offers 0% on balance transfers. The low introductory rate will only apply for a short time (for example, six months), but it'll give you some breathing space to get back on track and pay less interest for a while.

- *Consolidate your debt* – Another option is to transfer your card debt to another loan, such as a mortgage. It's not always a suitable strategy though, because instead of paying your credit card debt in the next few months, you'll be repaying it over 25 or 30 years. That means you'll pay much more interest in the long run. Furthermore, transferring the debt only really works if you cancel the old card – otherwise you could be tempted to start spending on it again. And watch out for the sharks circling vulnerable consumers in this area – dodgy loan brokers have been

FIVE SNEAKY TRICKS TO AVOID

We've read through the legal jargon of dozens of credit card contracts, battled with terms and conditions that at times seem designed to confuse, and analysed (in great detail) the variety of ways card companies charge interest and fees. But we're still surprised at the new ways they devise to charge customers even more, often in underhand and sneaky ways. Watch out for:

1 *Interest on late payments* – Many card providers use a variety of sly tactics to extract the maximum interest from customers who pay their bill late or not in full. They may cancel your interest-free days on new purchases if you don't pay your previous balance *in full* by the due date. When you pay *some* of your bill on time (but not the full bill), they'll charge daily interest, backdated to when the original purchase was made or when it hit your account.

2 *Cards that reduce interest-free days for 'always payers'* – In 2008 Citibank reduced the number of interest-free days for credit card customers who usually clear their bill each month. The change means that statements will be sent out ten days later than before, and customers will have fewer days after that to pay their bill. A Citibank customer told CHOICE, 'I could have my interest-free days lessened for what I regard as good behaviour – paying my credit card on time each month. To me

If you're in debt

'I always advise people who are carrying debt on several credit cards to clear the card with the smallest outstanding balance first, and then cancel the card. Keep paying minimum repayments on other cards. Then move on to the card with the second smallest balance, and do the same. This tends to work better than clearing the highest interest card first, because people achieve the first goal quicker – and feel like they're getting somewhere.' Katherine Lane, Principal Solicitor, Consumer Credit Legal Centre, NSW.

that is a worsening of conditions and therefore a penalty – and a sneaky way of gaining more money for the benefit of the bank and its shareholders.'

3 *BPAY traps* – Sometimes, if you use your credit card to pay bills via BPAY (a system for paying bills over the phone and online), the biller may treat the transaction as a cash advance, not a purchase. That means there's no interest-free period with your card, and fees apply. Check the policy of the company you're paying the bill to.

4 *Balance transfers* – There may be a sting in the tail when you transfer your card balance to a 0% introductory rate for six months – some T&Cs stipulate that any *new* purchases on the card will attract interest at the standard rate, and any repayments you make will be used to clear the 0% part of the balance before the part that's being charged high interest. Also, late payment fees (around $30) will be charged if you don't pay the minimum monthly repayment, even during the six month interest-free period.

5 *Cash advance interest* – From the bank's perspective, it's an 'oldie but a goody'. If you use your credit card for ATM withdrawals, interest applies from day one, and for every day until you repay the amount. What's more, the cash interest rate is often a per cent or two higher than the standard rate for purchases.

known to encourage consolidation which leaves customers with more problems than they had before.

- *Get help* – If you're struggling to repay your card debt, contact your card company to explain the problem and to ask about getting into a loan repayment plan. Talking to a financial or debt counsellor before the problem escalates is another excellent idea – check your phone book or enter 'financial counsellors' in the search box at <www.fido.gov.au>.

- *Use a debit card* – After working hard to get back on track, the last thing you want is to start the problem all over again by racking up new credit card debts. It could be time to get rid of your credit card and to use a debit card for purchases instead. It'll only let you spend what's in your bank account, and now MasterCard and Visa debit cards can be used for Internet and overseas purchases too, just like credit cards.

Do this TODAY *Compare your credit card's annual fees and interest rates with the best on the market. Cards are available with up to 55 interest-free days, competitive interest rates, and no annual fees. If your card doesn't match up, switch to a more competitive card and start saving now.*

STORE CREDIT AND LEASING

There's little doubt that easy credit has fuelled our spending boom. Our thirst for bigger TVs, home theatre systems and the latest electronic gadgets has been matched by a proliferation in the in-store finance deals available. Why worry about the cost of putting a $5000 cinema screen in your living room when you 'buy now, pay later' or 'try before you buy'?

In 2008 GE Money launched the ECO MasterCard. The company claimed that if you spend $600 per month on the card it'll offset the annual carbon emissions of the average Aussie. Sounds great – why not save the planet while indulging in a little retail therapy?

What happens is this: for each purchase you make with your card, GE uses 1% of the money to buy carbon offsets, which are designed to take greenhouse emissions out of the atmosphere or stop them getting there in the first place. So if you spend $600 per month, $6 will go towards offsetting emissions.

From a personal finance viewpoint, the card is comparable to rewards cards, though designed to reward the planet rather than provide you with flight points or retail items. The annual fee is $49 and interest rates are 18.49% for purchases and 19.99% for cash advances.

What then is the bottom line? You could be better off with a lower interest card and use the money saved from lower fees and interest to buy carbon offsets or renewable electricity. And it's always worth reading the fine print to fully understand the green claims being made.

Well, as the impact of the global recession is being felt by households, we may see the pitfalls of store finance come to the fore. Like credit cards, store finance deals can work for many people. It's all about using credit smartly and not letting it use you.

How store finance works

When buying an appliance, the shop may offer a 'buy now, pay later' deal to make it more affordable. You'll have to sign a credit contract, which usually involves an interest-free period of anything from twelve months to four years. During that time, you could choose not to make any repayments. But when the interest-free period ends, repayments are required at a predetermined rate. If you don't make your payments, watch out – you really will pay later, and pay dearly.

Another popular arrangement is where you pay for an item with regular interest-free instalments. You simply pay back the cost of the item back over a set timeframe. For example, a $1200 TV could be purchased with twelve monthly instalments of $120. No interest applies, unless you miss a payment, when interest rates approaching 30% per annum will be charged.

Good points
- If you're disciplined and make repayments when they're due, no interest applies.
- Store finance can enable you to stagger your payments for expensive items over a number of years, which may be good for your cash flow.

Bad points
- *If you miss repayments* on an interest-free program where you pay by instalment, interest applies, usually at a rate that makes credit cards look cheap. Expect to pay around 30% per annum on payments that are overdue.
- *Fees apply* – The standard monthly fee for these credit facilities is about $3 to $4, which adds to the cost of your purchase.
- *Interest-free finance* may encourage you to spend more than you can afford.
- *A new credit card* is usually part of the deal. The interest rate is likely to be higher than the best cards.
- *Check and negotiate the item's cash price first* – there's no point paying too much just because it's interest-free. You might get a better price for cash.

Renting and leasing

There are two main types of rental/leasing deals, and they're very different. Simple rental arrangements enable you to return the item any time you like at no cost. While the rental costs add up over time, these deals can suit some people – such as those in short-term house-sharing arrangements, who can split the cost of otherwise expensive appliances. If the fridge or TV breaks down, repairs may be included. Installation and servicing is often covered too.

Consumer leases are another type of rental deal, promoted in shops as an easy way to equip your home or office with the latest technologies and appliances, but they come with significant traps. Some of the contracts have proved expensive and problematic for consumers.

How leasing works

Usually, you sign up to a contract to make lease payments for a number of years. During that time you must pay a set amount each month. At the end of the lease period, you may be offered a choice of buying the item outright (for a fee to be determined at that time), upgrading to a new model, or just returning the item.

Bad points of leasing

- *High costs* – Lease payments can accumulate to 50–100% above the original cash price of the TV or fridge. You could own the item much sooner (with approximately similar monthly payments) by using interest-free finance instead.

- *Locked into a contract* – If you want to end the lease arrangement early, you may have to pay all lease payments anyway (or a high exit fee). It's not like simple renting, where you can just return the item at no cost when you're finished with it.

- *You may be obliged to pay lease payments no matter what happens* – even if the equipment is defective, lost, stolen, damaged or destroyed. Sometimes you have to pay for insurance – even though you don't own the item.

- *Often the consumer does not have the right to buy the item outright.*

- *Inadequate consumer protection laws* – These lease deals often aren't subject to regulations that apply to consumer finance and loans. The retailer or finance company isn't required to disclose the effective interest rate, or comply with the Consumer Credit Code that applies to loans and sale by instalment deals.

14

The mortgage meltdown

This economic downturn offers opportunities for some and big headaches for others.

Rampant house price inflation earlier in this decade saw homebuyers borrowing like never before. The traditional rule of thumb that people shouldn't pay more than one-third of their income on housing costs became irrelevant in many cases. In order to access properties that seemed to just go up and up, we needed to borrow more and more, and lenders were happy to provide the loans. But our wages didn't keep pace, which meant that our home-loan repayments, as a proportion of our income, became higher than ever before. While Australia never had the sub-prime or poor lending standards of the United States, we did see the advent of some 100% loan-to-value ratios and 'low-documentation' mortgages, which sustained and perpetuated the credit and property market bubbles at the margins. *Low-doc* loans are where the lender or broker doesn't require the full paperwork normally used to verify a borrower's income and capacity to repay the loan.

Then came the financial crisis. As property values around the world began to decline just like shares and other assets, property slowed in Australia too, though not as yet to the extent that we've seen overseas. Australia is one of the most expensive countries in the world to live in, when we compare the average house price with average earnings. Lots of people are saddled with huge debts over properties that have declined in value.

Add rising unemployment to that equation and it is no surprise that many are experiencing a mortgage meltdown. In early 2009, the research company Fujitsu Consulting was predicting that close to a million households were headed for severe mortgage stress. With unemployment predicted to increase and house prices in certain areas having declined in value, some people needing to sell could be faced with the looming problem of negative equity – where their loan is bigger than their property's value.

Thankfully for borrowers, significant interest rate cuts have eased the repayment pressure for many. If you managed to get through the period when standard variable interest rates were over 9%, you might now find yourself with some extra money, with official interest rates having declined by 4.25% between 2008 and mid-2009. This gives a great opportunity to get ahead on your repayments and save thousands of dollars in the long run.

The first section of this chapter looks at great home-loan strategies in a low-interest environment, and how to compare and find a good mortgage product. The second section looks at what you can do if the recession is putting you under mortgage stress and where to find more help and information.

TIME FOR A QUICK FIX?

The Reserve Bank of Australia reduced its target cash rate by 3% in late 2008 and by another 1.25% by April 2009. Once again, borrowings started to look cheap, with interest rates at 40-year lows. This environment could present a great opportunity to fix your home loan rate and lock in pretty low repayments. However, weigh up the pros and cons of fixing before deciding.

The first warning with fixing is that interest rate cycles are hard to predict and consumers often get it wrong. Interest rates are one of the policy levers used by governments to manage the economy (called monetary policy). When a government wants to prevent inflation for example, it may increase interest rates. When it wants to 'stimulate' the economy, encouraging us to spend more money and prevent the country from going into a deep recession (like we're seeing now) interest rates may be reduced.

The problem is it is very hard to predict major world events, such as the global financial crisis, and the effect they may have on interest rates at home. The graph on page 166 shows the dramatic increase in the number of people fixing their home loans between 2006 and 2008. Close to a quarter of new loans were being fixed in March 2008, when the Reserve Bank interest rate was 6.25%. Undoubtedly, borrowers felt that interest rates were going to go higher taking their mortgage repayments to unaffordable levels, so they moved to fixed rates as an insurance policy. But now, that's proving a costly decision. The graph shows how the present interest rates cycle peaked at 7.25% between March and August 2008, before declining rapidly. The upshot is that many people who fixed when rates were peaking are stuck in expensive loans. About 23.9% of loans were fixed in November 2007 when the RBA cash rate was 7.25%; by January 2009, a year later, less than 4% of new loans were being fixed, even though interest rates were 3% lower.

The dangers of fixing your mortgage

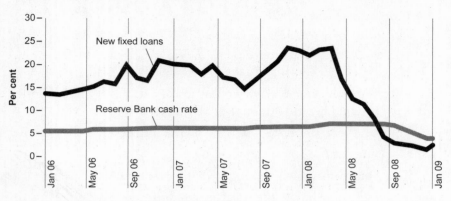

SOURCE Graph generated from ABS and RBA statistics

TRAPS OF FIXED LOANS

The downturn offers great opportunities to lock-in relatively low interest rates. However, borrowers should enter into fixed loans with their eyes open.

- *Break fees apply* – If you want to switch lender or end the contract for any reason, you'll have to pay a break fee. These fees are opaque and hard to calculate – they depend on a range of variables, which are changing all the time, including the remaining loan amount, fixed and variable rates when you took out the loan, and current rates. The people who fixed at relatively high rates in 2007 or 2008 are in the worst position; variable rates are now 4% lower but the break fee to exit fixed loans could cost tens of thousands of dollars.

- *Interest rates are hard to predict* – People who locked in to fixed contracts at around 8% or 9% probably thought rates were going higher. They were wrong and the error of judgement is now proving costly. The truth is, predicting interest rate cycles, like predicting stock market trends, is very difficult for amateurs. That's the sort of thing professional bond traders working for financial institutions do. That said, locking into a fixed rate at around 5% is more attractive than a couple of years ago at 9%.

But are you confident that interest rates won't go lower?

- *Can you make extra repayments?* – Fixed rate loans don't have the flexibility of variable rate loans. Most fixed loans don't enable you to make extra repayments, making it harder to fast-track your mortgage. Check your lender's rules before locking-in for a fixed period. Some allow you to make extra repayments up to a certain amount, such as $5000 each year.

All in all, if you want absolute certainty over your repayments for a certain period, fixed rates do that job. Whether fixed rate loans will save you money is less certain, because interest rates change and are hard to predict. A middle ground is to split your mortgage with both variable and fixed elements, so that you have some certainty but also a variable portion that allows you to make extra repayments. Essentially, you're hedging your bets.

CHOOSING A GOOD LOAN

This section looks at the main types of home loans on the market and what to factor into your decision. Ultimately, the best choice is the loan with the lowest interest and fees that also provides the features and facilities you need.

- *Standard variable* – the most popular type of home loan, this usually is pretty flexible, offering the ability to make extra repayments, and often extra features like a redraw facility or offset account (see below).
- *Basic variable* – a 'no frills' loan with an interest rate lower than the standard variable. Some basic loans don't allow extra repayments, however, and few have offset accounts and redraw facilities
- *Fixed rate* – you're guaranteed the repayments will stay at a set amount for a period of one to five years. Switching before the fixed term ends, and making extra payments, is usually penalised with a break fee.

- *Professional package* – for a fee of about $350 per year, you get a package with a reduced variable rate, a fee-free bank account and a credit card.

- *Redraw facility* – this allows advance payments you make to your loan to be withdrawn at a later date. A fee of around $50 usually applies.

- *Offset account* – all money that goes into the account offsets the loan balance on which interest is charged. For example, if your loan has a $200,000 balance, and you've $5000 in the linked offset account, interest would be calculated on $195,000. Make sure the account offers 100% offset and check for fees.

Before you borrow

Try to save at least 20% of the purchase price of your property, to avoid paying lender's mortgage insurance, which costs several thousand dollars.

Lenders' websites, mortgage brokers and others may say you can borrow loads. Do a stress test – what would happen in the case of a job loss, a new addition to your family, interest rate hikes or a serious illness?

Put your loan in the fast lane

If your loan has a variable rate, you've probably seen it reduce by about 3–4% in 2008 and 2009. For someone with a remaining balance of $300,000, the difference between paying 9% and 5% in interest alone could be $750 per month.

Lenders usually automatically reduce the monthly repayment to the lower amount when rates decline. But if you were able to manage when interest rates were higher, continuing to make that same higher repayment could take literally tens of thousands of dollars and years off your loan in the long-term. Because all the extra repayments you make will reduce the principal amount on which interest is calculated.

Fast-tracking your mortgage isn't complicated, if you have the cash. All it really involves is paying more money, more often. But there are a few tricks we can use to help us do this:

1 *Pay fortnightly* – Most people pay their mortgage monthly. But if you divide your monthly payment in two and pay fortnightly instead, you'll make a whole month of extra repayments each year. Why? Simply because there 26 fortnights, not 24, in a year. Just check this works for you from a cash-flow perspective (you may need to rearrange the timing of other bill payments, for example).

2 *Increase your regular repayment* – If you can go beyond paying the minimum, all extra repayments will come off the principal amount of your home loan. In turn, this reduces future interest payments, because the interest will be calculated on a smaller balance. The table on page 170 shows the effect of interest regular payments to a $300,000 loan that has 25 years left to run. Upping your monthly payment by $500 would take a whopping $112,000 and eight years off your loan, assuming interest rates don't change.

3 *Make lump-sum payments when you can* – If you have some spare cash, there are few better no-risk investments than your own home loan. It's like getting an investment 'return' equal to the loan's interest rate, and what's more, the return is tax-free. It'll also reduce your future interest payments, because the loan is smaller.

4 *Make extra repayment to the higher interest portion* – If your loan is split (for example, between variable and fixed portions), it's most beneficial to make extra repayments to the higher interest portion first. If that's the fixed loan, just check if there's a break fee charged for extra repayments (there usually is) and whether it's waived for a certain amount of extra payments each year.

Fast track your mortgage

Loan: Standard variable loan: $300,000 over 25 years at 6%					
Extra repayment per month ($)	50	100	150	200	500
Interest saved over 25 years ($)*	18302	34149	48932	60315	112300
Loan-term shortened by (years)*	1.4	2.7	3.8	4.8	8.11

* The calculations assume that interest rates don't change

Give your loan a health check

One of the many unwanted effects of the financial crisis is the loss of market share for non-bank lenders. While non-banks are often credited with introducing more competition to the Australian home-loan landscape in the 1990s, by 2009 their influence had waned and some had disappeared altogether. Their costs had increased and unlike banks and other Authorised Deposit Taking Institutions, they couldn't rely on savers to provide the funding for new loans. With non-bank lenders out of the way, the big banks began to take back market share. By 2009, the big four banks commanded up to 90% of the market for new home loans.

This is a concern for borrowers because it means less competition among lenders and could result in relatively more expensive loans for you. The big banks are getting bigger with Westpac's takeover of the fifth largest bank, St George, and Commonwealth Bank's merger with BankWest.

Despite the dominance of our largest four banks, there is still plenty of choice in the mortgage market. So if your lender isn't up to scratch, you could save money by switching to another provider. There's no harm in giving your loan a 'health check' to see how it compares. Here's what to consider:

- Interest rate is the biggest factor in the cost of your loan. As well as comparing the standard (nominal) interest rate, check out how 'comparison rates', which include the effect of fees and charges, compare.

- If you're on your lender's standard variable rate, you could be paying over the odds. Most lenders offer discounts of up to 0.7% off their standard variable rate to borrowers with loans above about $250 000.

- Do you need the bells and whistles? Offset accounts, redraw facilities, a line of credit and other facilities can save you money and provide convenience. But you usually have to pay for these facilities. Some people are better off with a simple basic variable mortgage that has a lower interest rate. But beware; some basic variable loans penalise you if you make extra repayments.

- Are you on a 'professional package'? For a fee of about $350 per year, banks offer packages that include a fee-free transaction account, gold credit cards, 100% offset account and a discounted interest rate. It's worth weighing up the pros and cons of these packages with what the benefits would be worth if you bought each financial product separately. A cost comparison by Canstar Cannex found that a customer with a 25-year home loan of $250 000, a gold card and a deposit account could save over $1000 a year with a bank's package deal, instead of buying each of these products separately from the same bank. However, it's worth shopping around different institutions for the cheapest cards, home loans and accounts – that may work out cheaper than giving all your business to one institution, even if you do pay for their package.

DEALING WITH MORTGAGE STRESS

Job loss and relationship breakdown are two of the biggest causes of mortgage stress. And while Australia has avoided some of the more severe problems experienced in the United States, there's no doubt that mortgage stress has increased here too. This could get worse before it gets better, particularly if unemployment rates escalate towards 8% or 9%.

If you've found yourself in this situation, there are steps you can take to alleviate the problem and find a solution. The earlier you recognise the problem and do something about it the better. Because when you start to miss repayments and get letters from your bank, your options start to reduce.

1 *Contact your lender* – As soon as you start to feel mortgage stress and think you're going to miss a repayment, it's important to contact your lender. You may be able to negotiate changes to help you cope. They may include taking a break from repayments (a payment holiday), extending the loan term (to reduce your regular repayments now), accessing equity that you've built up in the home, restricting the loan or even refinancing.

2 *Keep making whatever payment you can.*

3 *Know your rights* – The Uniform Consumer Credit Code (UCCC) allows those in temporary difficulty to extend their loan term to reduce regular repayments, and to postpone the date when payments are due. These are the hardship variations available under the Act, which have recently been extended to loans up to $500 000.

4 *Get free advice* – Financial counsellors provide free and confidential information. They can negotiate with lenders on your behalf, and ensure that the hardship provisions are made available to you. They can't provide legal advice, but can often refer you to a free service that can.

5 *What not to do, a warning* – Sadly, there are unscrupulous brokers that take advantage of people in mortgage stress while promising to help solve their problems. This may involve encouraging borrowers to refinance to a fringe or 'predatory' lender, while the broker charges huge fees – tens of thousands of dollars in some cases. The borrower is left in a much worse position than before the refinance – with the equity they'd built up in their home eroded and still with the real chance that they'll lose their home. Another tactic favoured by unscrupulous operators is to encourage consumers to withdraw their super to meet their loan repayments. While this is allowed under the legislation in some circumstances, it also often leads people into worse difficulties – losing both their home and their superannuation savings.

A SWITCHING CHECKLIST

Do your research – Use information websites like <www.infochoice.com.au> and <www.canstarcannex.com.au> to compare loans (the latter includes home loan 'Star Ratings' reports). Remember to include credit unions in your research, as they often offer the best value loans. You could also call a few mortgage brokers to see what they would recommend.

Contact your lender – to make sure you're on its most competitive deal. If you threaten to switch, your existing lender might shave some interest off your rate, or suggest a more cost-effective product to match a competing lender.

Check switching costs – In some cases, the exit fees from your existing loan make switching to another lender uneconomical. So-called 'deferred establishment fees' often apply if you leave a lender in the first few years. Fixed rate home loans can have significant exit fees. And check what establishment fees apply with the new loan, before making your decision.

Should you use a broker?

Mortgage brokers can help you compare lenders, work out how much you can borrow and assist with the loan application paperwork. This can save you time, particularly if you don't know your way around the mortgage maze.

However, there are a few things you need to understand about brokers. They're paid through commissions from lenders, so they've a potential conflict of interest – they may favour lenders paying higher commissions, and the more you borrow, the more money the broker makes. And brokers don't represent all lenders. Some lenders cut out the middle man and don't use intermediaries. Research by CHOICE found that mortgage brokers don't always have the cheapest lenders on their panels. It's worth checking out lenders that don't sell through brokers, including Internet-only banks, building societies and credit unions.

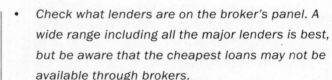

Using a mortgage broker

- *Check what lenders are on the broker's panel. A wide range including all the major lenders is best, but be aware that the cheapest loans may not be available through brokers.*
- *Check how the broker is paid and whether lenders that pay higher commissions are favoured.*
- *Don't pay fees to the broker.*
- *Get a broker agreement. It should disclose the broker's fees and commissions.*
- *Make sure your loan application and other documents are completed accurately.*

The good news for borrowers is that mortgage brokers will soon be subject to tighter consumer protection laws, requiring a license from ASIC and membership of an independent scheme for consumer complaints. Brokers will also be required to disclose their commissions, fees and lender panel up-front.

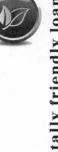

With concern for the environment rising, some lenders are offering 'green' options. For example, Bendigo Bank's Green Home Loan offers an interest rate of 0.5% below its standard variable for people installing things like double glazing, solar hot water heaters, water storage tanks and alternative forms of renewable energy generators, such as solar panels, wind turbines and small hydro power systems. The bank says it considers the reduced interest rate offered (therefore reduction in revenue) for the green loans as an investment in sustainable practice. 'We aim to develop initiatives that make being environment friendly also financially friendly,' Bendigo Bank says.

Environmentally friendly loans

15

Recession-proofing your job

Protecting your primary source of income should be first priority.

When economic times get tough, the number one way to recession-proof yourself is to keep your job. But there's no doubt that the job market is being squeezed, with layoffs and redundancies increasing. At the time this book went to print, the official unemployment rate was drifting towards 6% in Australia. Our unemployment rate is shown in the graph on page 177. An ANZ survey published in early 2009 found that the number of job advertisements being placed had fallen to 'recession levels'. Newspaper advertisements were down over 50% and job ads placed on the web were down 28%, in one year. Many stories have emerged of employees being asked to work four-day weeks to keep their job, as well as hours being cut and companies putting a freeze on replacing staff that leave or hiring for new positions.

There are some pretty gloomy predictions around what these statistics could mean for the employment market. Many believe that the jobless rate could increase to around 7% in 2009, and even

Australia's unemployment rate, 1978–December 2008

SOURCE Generated from ABS, Labour Force Australia, December 2008, Cat No. 6202

towards 9% by 2011. That would mean a million Australians out of work. And to some extent, the official unemployment figures don't tell the full story, because they don't account for the part-time workers who'd like to work more hours, for example. The Australia Institute, a think tank, reckons that for every one person recorded as officially unemployed, there are some 1.2 'hidden unemployed'. This would mean the 'real' unemployment rate is somewhere between 11% and 12%.

'2000 and 2001, when the "tech bubble" burst, was the last time the employment market was like it is now,' says Jacky Carter of Hays Specialist Recruitment. 'I've worked in recruitment for 22 years and

Job confidence hits a low

The Westpac/Melbourne Institute Consumer Sentiment Survey, published in February 2009, asked consumers how they feel about their job security. The index showed a deterioration of 59% over the previous year and the highest level of job insecurity since the survey began in 1974.

I can say that every recession is different. The downturn we're in now is more about consumer confidence and business confidence.'

To a large extent, we're part of an international trend and subject to forces beyond our control. Countries that officially went into recession have experienced far worse employment problems; in the last two months of 2008, a million jobs were lost in the United States and the UK labour market deteriorated rapidly too.

In most cases, there's little that employees can do to prevent redundancies happening within an organisation. However, there are early steps that you can take to ensure that you avoid the hit list if your organisation does need to scale back. They all revolve around making yourself valuable – even indispensable – to your employer. This first section of this chapter gives some great tips to ensure you're seen as a vital part of the team. The second part of the chapter looks at ways to manage a redundancy, and avenues to get more information.

ENSURING YOU KEEP YOUR JOB

Here are some thoughts about making sure your job is safe, as best you can.

1 *Increase your activity levels* – When times are tough, upping your productivity level is good for you and good for your employer. Of course, what you can do depends a lot on the type of role, but there are ways that many of us can work smarter and more efficiently. Do everything you can to ensure your job – and your organisation – remain successful. This doesn't necessarily mean working longer hours – it's about adding as much value as you can.

2 *Reduce cost / waste* – Many employers are looking to reduce their overheads. Think about ways that you can contribute to lowering costs and waste in your workplace. Question and challenge all

expenses. Think about whether expenditure is really necessary – would you spend the money if it was coming from your wallet?

Cutting costs will help the organisation's bottom line, which is good for everyone when money is tight. Make sure your employer or boss is aware of your efforts and initiatives. There are lots of ways to reduce cost and waste. If you work in an office, for example, could you and your colleagues use less paper, stationery and electricity?

3 *Take more responsibility* – Organisations now have to achieve more with fewer people. Volunteering for new responsibilities and duties beyond your usual role will help to demonstrate your commitment and value to the company through challenging times. Cross-skilling within the organisation can be a great idea for you – employees who have worked across a range of departments or organisational functions are often more valuable than those who really only know how to do one job. Demonstrate that you can adapt and change.

4 *Support organisational activities* – Most employers want to avoid redundancies and many are thinking about ways to get through difficult times without shedding staff. This may involve, for example, asking staff to take annual leave at a time of year when business is slow, or even asking staff to take unpaid leave. It may not be ideal for you, but consider supporting such activities in the long-term interests of your position and the organisation's viability.

5 *Be realistic* – Employment and recruitment consultants say workers need to be realistic about pay increases during a downturn. While the economy and jobs market soared, times were good and there was money in the kitty to reward staff through pay increases. In tougher times, such salary increases are less likely. This is a change for many younger employees who've never experienced a recession, but when the going gets tough, holding on to your job (job security) may be reward enough for your efforts.

6 *Have clearly defined job goals* – Have explicit work goals against which your performance can be measured. If you can demonstrate that you're meeting and even exceeding the goals that have been set for you, your employer will see that you're a valuable asset to hold on to. When push comes to shove, employees who are performing well are more likely to be retained.

Are there 'recession-proof' jobs?

Many companies will be forced to cut jobs to protect their profitability and improve their chances of surviving a global recession. But according to a research by IBISWorld <www.ibisworld.com.au>, some industries will escape relatively unscathed. The top 10 are:

- biotechnology
- online information services
- non-building construction (e.g. roads and bridges)
- cosmetic and toiletries retailing
- grain and livestock farming
- blood bank and health services
- Internet Service Providers
- passenger rail
- waste disposal services, and
- online shopping.

For every winner there will be losers. IBISWorld's list of industries least likely to provide new jobs and most likely to lay people off in the present downturn includes banking; tyre manufacturing; domestic airlines; boatbuilding and real estate agents.

7 *Find a mentor* – Look for people in your organisation that can give you advice and opinion about how you're performing, and ways that you can become more valuable to your employer. Your mentor could be a colleague or your boss.

8 *Join a union* – Trade unions can provide support and advice to members about their rights at work.

BE PREPARED FOR REDUNDANCY

You might feel perfectly secure in your job, but the reality is that in a downturn or recession many people will be laid off. The section 'If you're made redundant' on the next page looks at steps you can take after losing a job, but wouldn't it be better to have some contingency plans just in case this happens?

1 *Be proactive* – When times were good, prospective employers might have come looking for you. That's less likely now – you'll need to be more proactive in seeking out new opportunities.

2 *Look for training opportunities* – In downturns, there tends to be an increased emphasis on education, training and 'upskilling'. Enrolment in courses increases when people find themselves out of work – part of a redundancy payout may be used to develop your skills in a particular area, or even to branch out into a new area as the first step in a career change. Check out the skills and training levels of people in competing organisations. If you were to apply for a job with a competitor, would your skills measure up to what's expected?

3 *Update your resume* – Your CV is essentially like a personal marketing or business proposal document. Recruitment agents and outplacement companies can help you put a good one together.

4 *Start networking* – There's a whole network of professionals available, that many people don't know about. It could be a good idea

to network and make contacts with recruitment agents even if you feel pretty secure in your job – the relationships you form may come in handy later. Experienced recruitment consultants have expertise, don't cost anything for you, and have taken clients through previous downturns. Similarly, can you tap into business networking groups and alumni associations?

5 *Manage your online image* – Actively manage what you say and upload onto social networking sites (such as Facebook and MySpace). Assume that any new employer can access your profile, and they do with reports of employers 'googling' new candidates. But social networking and having an online presence isn't all negative – it could be worth starting up a profile to cast your net wider through a professional network site. LinkedIn is one of the best known of these sites. Other ideas include starting a personal blog, giving prospective employers an insight into your talents and personality.

IF YOU'RE MADE REDUNDANT

Get what you're owed

It's important to know your financial entitlements if you're laid off, to make sure you get what you're owed. Your final payout is a combination of your termination pay or severance, leave you haven't taken and superannuation entitlements. What you receive depends on the contract, award or agreement that covers your employment.

If you're a member of a union, it can help determine what you are entitled to. So can your employer or its human resources department. Otherwise you can contact the industrial relations department in your state or territory, or the Workplace Ombudsman.

A major insurance company is trialling an insurance policy that would pay out if the insured person was made redundant. It's too early to say whether the product will be fully rolled out, but it would certainly tap into a major consumer fear – that of a loss of income or employment.

Insure against losing your job?

Outplacement services

Before you leave check what additional assistance and services your employer is willing to provide. They may help you find a job, pay for training and career advice and put you in touch with an outplacement consultant to assist in your move. Make the most of these services and try to negotiate with your employer to receive as much help as you can after you've been made redundant.

Take care of your taxes

Unfortunately, tax applies even to redundancy payments. It's complicated enough as each part of your payout is taxed differently. Unpaid leave is taxed at a maximum rate of 30%. Severance payments are taxed separately; in general, a tax-free threshold applies. You won't pay tax on the first $7350 plus $3676 for each year of completed service, for the 2008/09 financial year. Payments above those amounts are taxed at various rates, depending on how much of the payment is from before July 1983, when the rules changed. For details, go to <www.ato.gov.au>.

It could be worthwhile to see a financial planner or tax adviser in relation to the best way to take severance pay. Some people could, for example, roll it into superannuation to defer the tax payment to a later date. A professional may also be able to advise on the most

The emotional impacts of recession

Research shows that losing a job or money can increase the risk of health problems, such as anxiety and depression. It's normal to experience a range of emotions in reaction to unexpected loss or changed circumstances, including shock, distress, anger, guilt, helplessness and sadness. There's not much you can do to change the state of the economy, but according to *beyondblue*, a national initiative to help people suffering from depression, there are practical steps you can take to gain control over your finances and well-being.

> 'Our infoline operators are seeing an increase in the number of callers experiencing stress due to financial downturn, job losses and even the fear that they could be next,' says Clare Shann, a psychologist and Acting Deputy CEO of *beyondblue*. 'People don't have control over whether they'll lose their job or the state of the economy, but research shows that a really important strategy in those circumstances is to look at what you can control.'

'Taking care of yourself after retrenchment or financial loss', a free booklet by *beyondblue*, is available at <www.beyondblue.org.au>. Contact details are also listed at the end of this book.

beneficial date to start your redundancy – for example, by taking remaining annual leave first and delaying the redundancy start date until after that, your tax-free payment for each year of service could increase.

Organising your finances

You'll probably need to re-jig your finances after a redundancy. Look at all the major components – your borrowing, investments, savings, insurance and super – to check what changes are needed. For example, you might struggle to pay the mortgage while you look for new employment – the bank might allow you to take a repayment holiday. You might end up without life, serious illness or permanent disability insurance after your employer stops paying the premium to your super fund – clarify the situation with your fund to ensure you don't go uninsured. You'll also need to consider the most appropriate place for your severance pay. It could be a bank deposit, your home loan, an investment fund or super. This could be a good time to get professional advice that's tailored to your individual needs.

Salary expectations

Be realistic about the salary you look for. Jobs are in high demand and employers are expected to trim costs, so be careful not to price yourself out of the market.

16

Slash your shopping bills

Easy ways to spend less money every week

Supermarkets have an intimate understanding of the psychology of shoppers, and use every trick in the book to get us to fill our trolleys and spend more money. Sweet baking smells near the entrance tempt us in and expensive non-essential items are placed at the cash register as we queue to get out. Special offers encourage us to buy two or three items when one would do, and treats such as biscuits are placed beside essentials like tea, a subliminal message to encourage us to buy both. Staples like milk and butter are situated at different ends of the same shop, increasing the chances that we'll fill our baskets with shiny goodies like soft drinks and chips en route. Supermarkets place the items they really want us to buy at eye level, hoping we'll miss the better value things above and below.

With the trend towards frugality and value hunting, you need to be armed with knowledge to defeat these retailers' tricks and avoid impulse buying. Here are our top tips to slash your shopping bills.

BEFORE YOU GO SHOPPING

With a little planning and research, there are ways we can all save money on groceries before we even leave home.

- *By making a list* – before you shop and sticking to it when you are out shopping, you'll just buy the things you need and avoid the non-essentials that add to your costs at the checkout. If you plan your week's meals prior to the shopping trip, you'll be less likely to buy expensive and often less healthy pre-prepared meals and processed foods.

- *Don't shop when you're hungry* – You'll be more likely to impulse buy and to purchase food that can be consumed on the spot, rather than better value alternatives.

- *Check catalogues* – Retailers bombard our letterboxes with brochures advertising their latest and greatest specials. Leaving aside the environmental impact of this enormous waste of paper (How often do you throw away the catalogue without opening it?), these brochures can help you to find weekly specials, vegetables in season and other bargains (for more information, go to the section on page 190, 'What's the best day to shop?').

- *Try Aldi* – The German-owned retailer cuts costs with a no-frills approach. It's far cheaper than Coles and Woolworths, especially for staples. If there's an Aldi in your area, try it.

- *Band together and hit the markets* – Wholesale markets are a great place for low-cost food. They often sell in fairly large quantities though, and you may not be wanting to buy 24 avocadoes at once. Why not get together with friends and neighbours to buy meat and vegetables in bulk at markets? You could take turns to do the market run for your mini shopping cooperative.

- *Shop later and not too often* – Late afternoons and evenings are often the best time to buy perishable items, as supermarkets mark down stock to get it off their shelves. Also, remember that more shopping trips could mean that you buy more items that you don't really need, and spend more overall.

Enter the 'value seekers'

Have we entered an era of thrift? A survey by the Australian National Retailers Association polled 1000 people about their spending intentions for the first half of 2009 and found that on average people were planning to cut their discretionary spending on items such as clothes, shoes, furniture and white goods by 21%.

But it's not just a case of cutting back. Nick Foley of the brand consultancy Landor Associates says the big trend for consumers is 'value seeking', where we expect not to have to pay full price, and we really question the value for money of all purchases. 'Value seeking and the desire for sustainability are the two most prominent consumer trends,' he says. 'When someone figures out how to combine those two trends they'll make a lot of money. It's the perfect storm.'

* *Leave the kids at home* – Admittedly, this tip won't be practical or possible for everyone, but it's clear that much of retailers' marketing efforts are directed at children accompanying parents on their weekly shopping trip. If you can't leave them at home, at least devise a good way to say, 'No'!

- *The downsizing trick is one of the latest retail traps to watch out for* – It happens when companies quietly change the size of the packets while keeping prices the same. If you use unit pricing, you'll be able to easily see the value for money.

- *Buying generic brands is another great way to save* – Research by Nielsen in 2009 has found that people are buying generic brands more. Particularly for staples, such as flour and sugar, you can save loads of money by buying home brands and white label products, without sacrificing on quality.

- *Buy in season* – Fruit and vegetables go up and down in price depending on when they're in and out of season. It's just supply and demand dictating the price. If you try to regularly avoid out-of-season items, you'll save loads of money in the course of the year.

- *Watch out for 'less than specials'* – The brand that's been reduced may still be more expensive than others. Consider whether offers like 'buy one, get one free' and 'two for $5' really represent good value, or just encourage you to spend and buy more than you need.

- *Check your receipt* – Sometimes items are scanned incorrectly or a special price isn't applied. It's worth having a quick look at your receipt to make sure. Any errors should be quickly rectified by the retailer.

- *Have your loyalty rewarded* – Loyalty cards from supermarkets' enable you to pick up points each time you shop at any of their stores. The points can be swapped for discounts or vouchers and other items later. Don't let the card dictate where you shop – for example, Aldi might still be the cheapest, even after bonus points from Coles and Woolworths are taken into account. However, if you shop in a number of different chains, there's no harm in having their cards in your wallet.

CASE STUDY
SAVE MONEY DURING EVERY SUPERMARKET VISIT

Ian Jarratt of the Queensland Consumers' Association is an expert on unit pricing and uses it to save money when grocery shopping. 'Having worked out price per unit of measure (unit price) for all sorts of grocery items, I've learned that unit prices can vary enormously,' Ian says. 'As a result, I have changed many previous assumptions about what will be the lowest unit price, for example that large sizes will always be cheaper than smaller, unpackaged will always be cheaper than packaged, and fresh will always be cheaper than frozen. I have found that these rules of thumb are often not correct.'

With compulsory unit pricing, consumers will be able to easily work out differences in unit prices and thus make better-informed decisions. Here are some of the ways Ian uses unit prices to save money:

- *Ham* – a small piece to slice at home is about half the price per kg of a pre-sliced package – about $10 rather than $20/kg.

- *Peanuts* – by buying loose per kg rather than in packets – about $7 rather than $10/kg.

- *Chicken breasts* – by buying loose at the deli rather than in prepacked trays in the chiller – about $11 rather than $15/kg.

- *Green beans* – by buying frozen rather than fresh in pre-packs – about $2 rather than $10/kg.

'Roll on compulsory unit pricing,' says Ian. 'I'll save even more money and lots of time.'

BUYING 'BIG TICKET' ITEMS

Of course, it's not just in supermarkets that you need to have your wits about you. For the new breed of value seekers, spending wisely on big ticket items like white goods and electronics is crucial too. We present here some tips regarding these purchases.

Don't bother with extended warranties

Salespeople often try to up-sell an extended warranty on our big ticket items. In most cases, the extended warranty is a waste of money. With a few exceptions, the majority of items we buy these days are pretty reliable and unlikely to break down. And everything you buy is covered by a legal 'implied' warranty anyway, meaning that for a while, the retailer is responsible for mechanical breakdowns or faults. For more information, go to <www.accc.gov.au>.

Haggle for the best price

The recession means it's a buyer's market. In a lot of cases, retailers have some flexibility to reduce their prices beyond what's advertised, and they'll do so to get a sale. This is true for everything from technology retailers to new car dealerships.

If you don't feel comfortable haggling, you could always ask the simple question, 'Is that your best price?' If you tell the salesperson that you're shopping around all competitors to find the best value, he or she may be more likely to give you their best deal.

Beware of cashback traps

There's been a big rise in the prominence of cashback deals, where shoppers are offered a discount some time after they purchase an item, if they complete a cashback voucher and return it on time. While the buying decisions of many are influenced by this clever marketing tool, research by CHOICE found that many shoppers run into difficulties too. Valid claims are denied or rejected for being too late, consumers have to jump through hoops to get paid, and claims can take months to process.

Pay in cash

You might get a discount for paying in cash, as the retailer doesn't have the extra costs associated with processing credit and debit cards transactions, or the wait for a cheque to clear.

Shopping with a conscience

The last few years have seen an increase in consumers wanting not just the best products and value, but to know that their money is being used in an ethical way. So we have 'fair trade' coffee, environment-friendly kitchen cleaners, green cars and more and more organic food.

But with some many labels and environmental claims, it's really hard for consumers to know who to trust. For a guide on how to make your green dollars really count, check out Tanya Ha's book The Australian Green Consumer Guide, *and websites like <www.acfonline.com.au> and <www.choice.com.au/green>.*

But there are also signs that consumers are starting to suffer from 'green fatigue', as it seems every type of product and service is advertised as having some environmental or socially responsible benefit. 'Greenwash' has been a rising problem – where marketers make dubious environmental claims to sell more products. It will be interesting to see if cash-strapped consumers continue to pay a premium for green products and services through this economic downturn, particularly if the price of pollution is priced into everyday items as a result of the government's climate change legislation.

What are my rights if a company goes bust?

During an economic downturn, an increase in the number of retailers, manufacturers and other companies going bust is inevitable. But what happens if you're owed money or another service, such as the replacement of a faulty appliance, repairs under a warranty agreement, or a cashback refund?

Unfortunately, when a business enters administration or receivership, customers may be regarded as unsecured creditors. Such customers are often among the last to get paid when a company collapses. Secured creditors, such as banks who loaned money to the business, as well as employees and suppliers, would usually receive at least a portion of what they're owed first.

As federal company law applies in these circumstances, state fair trading and consumer affairs offices are unable to help with refunds. Consumers should contact the Administrator or Receiver that has been appointed to the company that has stopped trading, and if unsuccessful, contact the Australian Securities and Investments Commission on 1300 300 630.

However, the news may not be all bad if you paid for the goods or service with your credit card or some types of debit cards. A system called chargeback may entitle you to a refund from your card provider, if you used your card to pay for goods or services that weren't received. Time limits may apply for claims; contact your card provider for more information.

Don't feel pressured

Have you ever found that you made a buying decision you later regretted, because you were pressured by a salesperson? Remember, it's your money and the salesperson, not you, is desperate for the transaction to go ahead. Take your time. If you feel too pressured walk away and think about it some more, and do some extra research if you need to. Chances are if you return to the shop the next day or the next week, the item will still be there.

Think about quality

We're all thinking about ways to cut our spending, but sometimes this can go too far. There's little point in buying a cheap TV that lasts two years, as you'll have to fork out more money to buy a better set later. But at the same time, a high price doesn't mean the best quality! Independent product tests by CHOICE regularly find

'Confusopoly' and the paradox of choice

One of the ironies of all the shopping choice we have these days is that when we're faced with so many options, we tend not to make any decision at all. One behavioural study found that when given a choice of 6 types of jams to taste, 30% consumers went on to purchase one of them. However, when shoppers were given a choice of 24 jams, just 3% followed through with a purchase.

And then there's the issue of 'confusopoly', a phrase coined by Scott Adams, the man behind the Dilbert comic strips. He defined confusopoly as 'a group of companies with similar products who intentionally confuse consumers instead of competing on price'. In Australia, mobile phone plans seem to illustrate confusopoly at work. Have you ever tried to compare the various operators' deals to find the best value? It's next to impossible. An ex-CEO of a major New Zealand telecoms company came close to admitting that the industry intentionally confuses consumers, when she said that for years telecoms companies around the world had been using confusion as their chief marketing tool!

that best performing appliances and other consumer goods aren't necessarily the most expensive. Check out <www.choice.com.au> for a wide range of products tests and to get the best value and quality items.

Convenience has a high price

Try to avoid picking up items at convenience stores and petrol stations. They have longer opening hours, but shoppers pay a significant price for this convenience.

17

Slash your household expenses

There are many ways to cut expenses to help your bottom line.

The easiest way to whip your personal economy into shape is to reduce what you spend. Some changes are easy – those items that you know are a waste of money before you've reached for your wallet. But cutting other expenses from your life will be harder and will require some sacrifices.

Nobody can really tell you what you *should* do to cut your expenses – that's really up to you. Of course we all have our weaknesses – some people might say pay TV and takeaway meals are easy ways to slash your bills, but some of us couldn't imagine being unable to indulge in the occasional Thai or pizza home delivery while watching the movie channel or live European football. You may not have to go without those things completely if you can limit what they cost.

This chapter gives you some ideas for saving money inside the home and when you're out and about. We also give tips on where you can go for more free money-saving information.

ENERGY BILLS

Energy costs are increasing and they're going to become a bigger expense for most households. Significant increases in electricity tariffs are being approved and climate change legislation will add the price of greenhouse pollution to our electricity bills. While some households will be compensated for this increase in costs, cutting your energy use will save you further money. The most effective way to cut your electricity and gas bills is to use less.

- *The first step is to properly insulate your home* – to keep in the heat in winter and to make sure the house keeps cool in summer. Roughly one quarter of household energy bills are for heating and cooling.
- *Air conditioners are among the worst energy guzzlers* – Set them at the optimum temperature (18–20°C in winter and 25–26°C in summer) – for every degree above or below that optimum, your electricity costs increase by up to 15%.
- *External shading over your windows in summer can keep the inside cool.*
- *Make the most of natural sunlight* – Turn off lights when you leave the room and use long-lasting energy efficient light bulbs.
- *Only heat the room that you're in.*
- *Install an energy-efficient showerhead* – Look for an AAA-rated model.
- *Use smaller appliances.*
- *Check your freezer is set at the most efficient temperature* – usually about –18°C. Make sure the fridge is placed away from sunlight, and has room around it for air circulation if possible.
- *Choose energy efficient appliances* – Check the energy star on the sticker – the more stars, the more energy efficient it is.
- *Turn off appliances at the wall whenever you can* – for example, wide screen TVs use a lot of power even when on standby. You

can see how efficient various appliances are when on standby in the product tests at <www.choice.com.au>.

- *Electricity companies charge for peak and off-peak use* – with peak rates being up to 62% more than the off-peak charges. 'A simple change in your daily routine, such as running the dishwasher and washing machine during off-peak hours, can save a lot of energy and money, according to the savings website the Cheapskates Club <www.cheapskates.com.au>. 'Fill the washing machine and dishwasher before you go to bed and set your alarm for 5 am and get up, hit the on button and go back to bed. If you can't face getting up early enough, then try programming the appliances to start automatically during the off peak time.'

TELECOMMUNICATIONS

Home phone, Internet and mobile costs comprise a large chunk of many households' monthly bills. Here are a few tips:

- Consider a bundled deal with one telephone provider for discounts.
- Ensure the mobile tariff plan you're on is suitable for your calling patterns. For example, some give a free amount of talk time – but if you're a heavy user of texts messages a plan to suit those needs could be more suitable.
- Capped mobile phone deals can limit what you spend each month if you're disciplined. But try not to exceed the cap, because excess usage fees apply. Again, make sure the plan and call spend included is good value for your needs.
- The big telephone companies often give discounts and free calls when you call another phone within the same network. It might make sense to get on the same network as the family members and friends that you call most often.
- Avoid premium rate mobile services – they're expensive.
- Shop around for the best phone and Internet rates and compare deals at <www.phonechoice.com.au>.

Most states in Australia now have retail energy competition, meaning you may be able to switch retailer for a cheaper deal. This won't affect the supply of electricity or gas to your home – only the company sending you the bill, your contract and the costs should change. The websites <www.choiceswitch.com.au>, <www.goswitch.com> and <www.switchselect.com> can help you compare offers and hopefully find a better deal.

Compare energy providers

BUY AND SELL SECOND HAND

We've always had op shops, classified ads and garage sales, but the Internet has opened up a whole new market for the buying and selling second hand items. Exchanging second hand items is good for the environment (less waste going to landfill) and good for your finances. Check out websites like <www.ebay.com> and <www.gumtree.com>. Selling unwanted items online – furniture, appliances, books, you name it – is also a great way to de-clutter your home. 'Walk around your house and make a list of things you don't use or don't need and sell them,' recommends the website <www.simplesavings.com.au>. 'Put the money towards your debt and don't be tempted to waste more money on clutter.'

EVERYDAY BANKING

A March 2009 study by Fujitsu Consulting found that Australians have among the most expensive banking services in the western world. With household budgets under pressure, it's important to minimise what you pay to access your money, make bill payments and other everyday banking activities. Here are our top tips.

1 *Only use your own bank's ATMs* – When you check your balance or withdraw cash from another financial institution or company's Automated Teller Machine, their ATM fee applies. It's usually about $2 per transaction, so one foreign ATM withdrawal per week would add up to more than $100 per year.

2 *Consider a package deal* – If you have a home loan, you may benefit from a professional package with the same institution. This usually includes a fee-free bank account (again, some transactions aren't included), a credit card and an offset account for your mortgage. The cost is usually around $350 per year, so weigh up that fee with the cost of buying the banking products you need separately.

3 *'All you can eat' accounts* – Most of the banks offer an account where for a set fee of about $5 per month you can make as many transactions with that institution as you like. But note, some transactions, such as foreign ATM withdrawals, aren't included.

4 *Avoid penalty fees* – Every time you overdraw your account or have insufficient money in your account to cover direct debits and cheques, you may be charged around $30.

5 *Consider a credit union* – Mutual societies such as credit unions often beat the big banks for customer satisfaction. They are community-based organisations owned by their members.

CAR, HOME AND TRAVEL INSURANCE

With all types of insurance, it really pays to shop around for the best deal. CHOICE comparisons regularly find the difference between the best and worst value policies is hundreds of dollars.

• The under-insurance of home and contents is a big problem so this is not a cover that you should skimp on, particularly given the extreme and harsh climate in our country. We don't need to be reminded of the terrible destruction that bushfires and floods have caused. For contents, go through each room in your house and try to calculate approximately what it would cost to replace each item. For building insurance, use an online calculator supplied on many insurance company websites to assess the value of your house.

- Consider bundling your policies with one insurance company to save on premiums.

- With travel insurance, avoid travel agents as they usually add significant mark-ups to the insurance price. You can often save money by buying from an insurance company or agent online. You could try to haggle or bargain with the travel agent for a better price. Beware that the very cheapest policies and insurance provided with gold credit cards may not be adequate. Read the terms and conditions and check if pre-existing medical or health conditions are covered.

- Think twice before taking out insurance policies you may not need. That may include credit card payment protection, rental car excess insurance (it might be covered for a lower premium through travel insurance), extended warranties for used cars and household appliances.

SAVING ON HEALTH INSURANCE

In previous recessions, some people have dropped their private health insurance, considering it a discretionary expenditure. Hospital and extras insurance isn't compulsory – everyone is entitled to treatment in a public hospital at no cost. However, private health insurance can give you a choice of doctor, cover for some of their fees and pay for private hospital expenses. You may also enjoy shorter waiting times for elective surgery (operations for conditions that aren't immediately life-threatening but can be painful and debilitating – such as cataract

**Reducing
your
health
cover
costs**

- *Pay annually – discounts and rate protection can reduce your premiums by around 4%%.*

- *Some funds give another 4% discount if you pay by direct debit.*

- *Some funds let you prepay the following year's premium up until 31 March – just before the annual premium increases come into effect.*

- *Choose to pay an excess on claims. That will reduce the premium you pay, but when you claim you'll have to pay the first several hundred dollars of the cost of the treatment. Just be careful that the excess isn't so high that it disqualifies you from being exempt from the Medicare levy. The excess limit is $500 for singles and $1000 for families.*

- *A few companies allow co-payment arrangements, whereby you have to cover part of the cost of treatment if you go into hospital, but you pay lower premiums as a result. But beware, there isn't usually an annual limit to what you may have to pay.*

- *Consider cancelling your extras cover, which pays for things like dental visits and physiotherapy. Frills and extras may not be worth the cost, particularly when money is tight. Hospital cover, on the other hand, doesn't tend to have bells and whistles.*

- *Don't pay for cover you don't need. If you're not going to have a baby, for example, why pay the premiums to cover it?*

- *Consider the waiting periods that apply when you join a fund. For example, if you know you're going to need eye surgery, be aware that after you take out hospital cover, a one year waiting period usually applies for pre-existing conditions before you can start to claim expenses.*

- *Compare cover and premiums. There are wide differences. Research by CHOICE has found that the 'best buys' can save you between $300 and $800 per year, depending on the cover chosen.*

- *Remember, saving money isn't everything – policies with lots of exclusions are sometimes to be avoided.*

  Thanks to <www.ozecover.com.au> and <www.choice.com.au> for some of these tips.

surgery or a hip replacement). Another type of policy – extras (ancillary) cover – helps you with the cost of medical treatment that isn't covered by Medicare, including physiotherapy, optical and dental visits.

The Government has introduced several incentives to encourage us to buy hospital insurance. There is a medical levy surcharge if you don't buy private health insurance (expected to be 1%–1.5%) plus rebates on premiums of 20%–30%, depending on your income. Under Lifetime Health Cover, people who start hospital insurance in their thirties or later pay more than those who arrange insurance earlier. If you are aged 31 or older and haven't already signed up for health insurance, you'll pay higher premiums than someone who joined at age 30 or younger.

The ins and outs of health insurance are complicated – there are lots of factors to consider, such as which hospitals are covered and which treatments are excluded. The section on page 204 gives tips on how to save money on your health cover – for a comprehensive guide to everything you need to know, check out <www.choice.com.au>, <www.ozecover.com.au> and <www.privatehealth.gov.au>.

COOKING AT HOME

The website <www.simplesavings.com.au> provides some good tips for saving on food bills at home. It recommends cooking from scratch, avoiding pre-packaged and pre-made meals and treats, and searching the Internet for cheap, nutritious recipes. Make a menu plan and stick to your shopping list for the ingredients.

Pack your lunch

It's easy to be tempted to buy lunch from a café or restaurant near work, but the costs add up. Bringing your lunch to work is guaranteed to save you money.

TRAVEL EXPENSES

Think about ways to save on petrol, motoring and other regular travel expenses:

- *Use petrol discount vouchers from supermarkets* – But watch out for false economies make sure the petrol station and supermarket are still good value! There's no point driving out of your way to save a few cents, if you could pay less at a shop or station that doesn't participate in the discount scheme.

- *Time your petrol fill up* – Tuesday is often the cheapest day. Go to <www.motormouth.com.au> for the best value in various cities.

- *Think about ways to avoid driving* – Can you walk, cycle, use public transport or car pool with friends and colleagues?

TAKEAWAY FOOD

Try to ensure that outsourcing your cooking is an occasional treat, but not the norm. There are easy ways to reduce the cost too, without having to go cold turkey. For example, when ordering Asian food, cooking your own rice could save $3 or $4. And instead of home delivery, you might save another $5 by picking up the meal yourself.

DO IT YOURSELF

Plumbers, painters and electricians can cost a fortune, so could make big savings by carrying out basic repairs and improvements around the house yourself. If you're a novice try a handyman class – hardware shops often run free classes at weekends covering things like painting and laying tiles. 'Changing tap washers, re-caulking tubs and toilets, changing fuses, replacing air filters, stopping leaky taps, blocking air leaks, and cleaning filters will save hundreds of dollars on your utility bills each year,' according to <www.cheapskates.com.au>.

HAVE A CHEAP NIGHT OUT

Check out the cheap night at your local cinema, look for discount vouchers in newspapers and free guides and check out online discount websites for vouchers and bargains. A word of warning though: some of these vouchers encourage you to spend money to save money. For example, a voucher might give you 10% off the entrance to a museum, but if you weren't planning to go there anyway, is the voucher making you spend, rather than save money?

18

Life and income protection insurance

*Protecting your wealth is
as important as building it.*

It may not be as exciting as investing or buying your own home, and frankly, few of us like talking about the possibility of getting sick or worse, but life and income protection insurance can be crucial components of a good financial plan. In fact, it is mandatory for financial advisers to address clients' life insurance needs. But despite their need for insurance, vast numbers of consumers, who may otherwise be on top of their finances, have inadequate protection.

The answers to a few simple questions may give clues as to whether you're adequately insured: if you became ill and were unable to work, would you (or somebody close to you) have enough money to cover your household expenses and medical bills while you recovered? And if you were to become permanently disabled or if you died, would your dependents be in a position to replace your income and clear your debts?

Many people would answer in the negative to these questions. And while under-insurance is a big problem in Australia, there's lots of unnecessary cover being bought too. With purse strings across the country being tightened, one of the best ways to reduce your monthly expenses is reducing the price of the insurance you need to buy. The key is in striking the balance between having enough life insurance at the right price, and paying too much for cover that isn't necessary. This chapter gives you some pointers.

LIFE INSURANCE

This insurance is more accurately known as 'death cover', because the only time it's paid out is when the policyholder dies. The sum insured is paid as a lump sum to the policyholder's estate or beneficiaries – whoever was nominated on the relevant forms. Death cover applies up to a set age – for example 65.

And as with the other types of life insurance, such as income protection and permanent disability, the price of death cover is influenced by a range of factors including:

- *your gender* – women generally live longer than men, so their premiums are cheaper

- *your age* – the older you are, the more you pay or the less cover you get

- *your health* – and whether you smoke

- *your occupation* – there premiums differ depending on the risks associated with your profession or occupation. Somebody who works at a desk in an office is at less risk than a person working on construction sites, for example

- *history* – of family illnesses

- *the results of any medical tests* – you've undertaken, including, for example, genetic tests which could indicate that you're genetically predisposed to certain illnesses such as breast cancer

- *your lifestyle* – or activities may be taken into account.

The level of life insurance you need really depends on your personal circumstances. Somebody with no dependants may not need any life cover, but income protection insurance could be vital. On the other hand, somebody who is the main breadwinner, with a spouse and children reliant on their income, may need substantial life insurance and income protection insurance. Another example of someone who could need cover is a younger person whose parents went guarantor on a home loan − if the borrower was unable to repay the loan because of death or disability, the parents would be left with the debt.

You may need to get advice about the right level of cover for you, and this can change over time. As an illustrative example, Frank Gayton, who heads up Industry Funds Financial Planning, says that somebody with a family and a mortgage might need enough life insurance to pay off the house if they die, and to provide about seven times their annual salary as a lump sum to dependents too. So if they have $200 000 remaining on their home loan, and an after-tax salary of $50 000, that person might require $550 000 of insurance.

Another very general 'rule of thumb' − at best a ballpark figure − is to buy cover of ten times your income. So somebody taking home $50 000 a year might buy $500 000 of cover.

However, needs vary widely so give your insurance needs careful consideration and consider speaking to an adviser. The cover you need is impacted by existing assets and investments you and your family have (which may reduce the cover required) and future anticipated expenses including debts and living costs (which increases your insurance requirements). Canstar Cannex has a life insurance cover calculator that can help you work out your needs, but stresses that you should also see an adviser to get the appropriate cover.

PERMANENT DISABILITY INSURANCE

Another type of life insurance – permanent disability – pays you a set amount if injury or illness leaves you disabled and unable to return to work. It's often sold as part of the package with death cover – for example, through super funds.

Make sure your policy covers both accident and sickness, and is appropriate for your occupation. It's also important to ensure that the policy is 'Guaranteed Renewable' – meaning that once the cover is taken out, the insurance company can't alter the policy or what it covers without your consent, even if your circumstances change or your heath suffers a setback.

INCOME PROTECTION INSURANCE

Income protection insurance is designed to temporarily replace your income, or a significant portion your wages, if an illness or injury means you're unable to work for a while. Unfortunately, income replacement cover is not intended to cover you if you're made redundant or get the sack. A few insurance companies, however, offer policies that can soften the financial blow of a redundancy by cancelling the premiums you have to pay for up to three months if the policy has been going for at least a year. Read the fine print to check companies' policies on this matter.

The maximum income protection insurance payout is about 75% of your salary. Like death insurance, the price of income protection depends on a range of factors, including your age, health and occupation. The 'waiting period' to receive payments after a claim, that you choose, also affects the price. For example, if an injury forced you to miss work, would you need to start receiving the insurance payments straight away or within, say, a month, or would you have enough emergency funds, sick leave pay or family support to tide you over for 8–12 weeks? The longer you'd be prepared to wait before the insurance payouts start coming in after a claim, the cheaper the premiums are.

When considering the amount of income protection you need, think about your existing expenses (mortgage, other loans, living costs, family costs) and what you'd need if you were unable to work for a period. Consider getting an 'index-linked' policy, where your premiums, and the payout you'd receive for a claim, rise over time in line with inflation. A non-cancellable policy could also be an idea; with other policies, the insurance company can reassess your health and other factors at the time of each renewal, possibly raising your premiums or refusing to continue cover if your health has changed.

Some income protection policies contain an 'offset clause', which means insurance payouts are reduced if you also receive other money from Centrelink or your employer.

SERIOUS ILLNESS (TRAUMA) COVER

Also known as 'critical', 'serious' or 'specified' illness insurance, it was invented by a doctor in South Africa in the 1980s. The cover pays you a lump sum if you contract a specified illness, or if a specific injury or illness is diagnosed. About 30 conditions are usually covered, with cancer, strokes and heart attacks the most common reasons for claims. Premiums for this type of insurance are comparatively expensive.

Protect your super contributions too

Some super funds enable you to arrange income protection insurance to replace up to 85% of your salary, with an extra 10% being directed to your superannuation investments, so your retirement nest egg continues to be topped up while you're off work. That means that while you're unable to work and not getting a pay cheque from your employer, contributions to your superannuation investments will continue.

WHAT DOES IT COST?

The price of insurance varies depending on your individual circumstances and needs, For the full suite of comprehensive cover – death cover, total and permanent disability, income protection insurance and trauma, Zurich Insurance says you could pay between 2% to 5% of your income. We asked Canstar Cannex to estimate what a man aged between 35 and 45 would pay for various types of cover. The table opposite shows the results, with the average price from a range of insurers. You'll need to do your own comparison for your specific circumstances; this table is just to give a feel for the costs.

Life cover

- As a rough guide, life insurance might cost around 0.1% of the amount insured per year, or 1% of your annual salary. That estimate is based on a 40-year-old in an occupation that has a 'standard' risk rating.
- Including total and permanent disability in the cover increases your costs.

- Depending on your circumstances, that may either seem like a waste of money or (for example, someone who doesn't need death cover as they've no dependents) or a necessary investment (for someone with a spouse and children, a mortgage and other and expenses). If you have dependents or a family, think about how they'd cope without your income.

- Another thing to remember is that increasing your level of insurance from your present amount doesn't have to be very expensive. Check it out.

Income protection

- Premiums vary, but about one week's salary per year is a general guideline for the cost of income protection insurance. Another estimate is about 1% to 2.5% of your salary to provide 75% income replacement.

- Similar to life insurance, factors influencing the cost of your income protection cover include your age, gender, health, if you smoke, occupation and the time you're prepared to wait for payments.

How much do wealth protection products cost?

Life Insurance			Income Protection*			Life and income protection
Amount of cover	Average monthly premium	Average annual premium	Monthly benefit	Average monthly premium	Average annual premium	Combined average annual premium
$350 000	$33.46	$401.50	$2200	$60.23	$722.70	$1124.20
$550 000	$44.71	$536.55	$3500	$90.64	$1087.70	$1624.25
$750 000	$57.79	$693.50	$4700	$113.15	$1357.80	$2051.30
$1 000 000	$69.96	$839.50	$6300	$140.83	$1689.95	$2529.45

All premiums based on averages across the industry for a 35–45-year-old male, non-smoker, white collar, stepped premiums, paid annually, as at 23 March 2009.
* Income Protection is based on agreed value, a 30-day wait, with the benefit paid to age 65.
SOURCE <www.canstarcannex.com.au>

- *Super funds often sell income protection in units* – with each unit providing $500 of cover per month. In that scenario, one unit would be insufficient for many people to meet their monthly expenses and loan repayments, so they'd need to buy more units. If the policyholder was prepared to wait 90 days instead of 30 days to receive the payments, the premium for the income replacement insurance would be approximately halved.

- *Income protection* – is often more expensive than life insurance, but you can claim a deduction for the premiums you pay, on your tax return. On the downside, if you're paid out an income protection insurance claim, it's counted as income so tax applies.

Are you under-insured?

There's considerable concern that people have inadequate levels of life and income protection insurance, particularly given our high debts and high cost of living. With many households having two working partners, with both salaries needed to keep up with mortgage repayments and many other expenses, the worry is that if one partner was unable to work, the whole financial situation would quickly unravel. Ill health and the death of a family's main breadwinner are among the major reasons for defaulting on loans. According to the Investment and Financial Services Association (IFSA), if one of the working parents of a two-income household was to suddenly fall ill or die, many families would struggle with the debt burden that would leave them having to reassess their living arrangements and children's education.

Data from Rice Warner Actuaries shows that the average life insurance cover per head for the working population is $181 000, or just under three years of average earnings. Of course, lots of those people may not need life insurance (if they don't have people who are financially dependent on them), but they may benefit from income protection and disability cover. Rice Warner projects that life cover

For the average 31-year-old male, married with two children and earning $75 000 per year, $750 000 of life cover and $4700 per month of income protection insurance costs an average of $2.83 per day, or just over $1000 per year.

Source: Investment and Financial Services Association, July 2007.

Cover might be cheaper than you think

will more than double in the next fifteen years, as more people become aware of the need for insurance, innovation and competition in the industry increases, buying insurance whether through an adviser or direct becomes easier, and super funds increase the default number of insurance units provided to members.

Do you have too much or too little insurance?

Now is as good a time as any to look into whether you have the appropriate level of life insurance for your circumstances.

While underinsurance is often cited as a major shortfall in individuals' financial planning, the flip side of the coin is that some people are paying for insurance they don't really need. Research by the Australian Institute of Superannuation Trustees (AIST) and Industry Funds Forum (IFF) found that while 51% of the 2000 individuals surveyed had death cover that was insufficient by $100 000 or more, 15% of people were actually over-insured by $100 000 or more.

Over-insured people include those paying premiums for death cover even though they've no dependents. If they were to die, would the payout really be needed? Another area of excess insurance is where people are doubling up by having a policy from two separate super funds, when one would be enough. And finally, some older people who've cleared their mortgage and are close to retirement and believed to be paying for death insurance that they (or more to the point, their dependents) do not necessarily need.

But people are far less likely to be over-insured when it comes to income protection insurance. AIST and IFF found that just 3% of those surveyed had too much income replacement insurance, compared to the majority (65%), who are under-insured for income protection insurance by $1000 or more per month. Coverage levels for total and permanent disability are even worse, with an estimated 71% under-insured.

How to get the best value

About two-thirds of life insurance is sold through super funds. And they are often the best value option for consumers. Superannuation funds have huge buying power, so they can negotiate good rates with insurance companies and offer reasonably priced premiums to their members. In many cases, you won't need to fill out detailed medical questionnaires or have a medical examination if the cover you need is less than about $600000 and you haven't had significant medical problems in the past. So before checking out other options, check out your super fund's rates – they're usually hard to beat.

Paying for insurance through super can also be a very tax-effective strategy. If your employer pays money into your fund (the 9% Super Guarantee payment), this comes from your pre-tax salary. Contributions to super are taxed at 15%. That means you'd probably pay less tax than if you took the same amount of money as an after-tax salary and used it to buy life insurance outside of super.

However, when insurance death cover is bought through super, there can be delays in dependants receiving the proceeds. That's because the insurance company pays the super fund's trustees, and

Individual, professional advice from a financial planner can help you assess your needs and identify suitable products and providers. It's important to know what types of products and companies the planner can advise on, and whether the advice may be influenced by the payments and commissions the planner receives from insurance companies. Chapter 11 'Getting expert advice' explains some of your options.

get ADVICE

it's up to the trustees to handle the claim and make the payment to the dependants of the insured member.

You could also buy life insurance through a financial planner or life insurance agent. However, there is a big trap: the commissions that pass between insurance companies and advisers can be pretty extraordinary. For example, the adviser might receive up to 130% of your first year's premium (that is, a payment equal to the first fifteen months of what you pay), plus an ongoing commission of 10% to 30% of your premiums in subsequent years. Remember, while the commission is paid to the adviser by the insurance company, not you, these costs will be indirectly passed on to you and are likely to be reflected in higher prices for insurance.

A fee-for-service financial planner, who doesn't get paid by commissions from financial institutions or insurance companies, may be able to rebate any commissions and kickbacks to you, just charging you directly for advice about your insurance needs.

Another avenue for buying life insurance is directly 'over the counter' from insurance companies. While you may not need to fill in a medical questionnaire to get the level of cover you need, the premiums may be higher than insurance through super in some cases.

Don't cancel cover without thinking it through

Chris Rutherford, Life Insurance Operations Manager with Zurich, points out that somebody who cancels life or income protection insurance may find it more difficult and expensive to resume cover later. 'Think about the health tests you did before, and whether you'd achieve similar results now and in the future if you took the tests again. You may not have needed to do any tests before because of your age but you may need to do them next time you apply.' Rutherford says. 'Premiums can increase if your health or history of medical problems changes or deteriorates. It's also important to think about the reasons you bought cover in the first place, and whether those needs have really changed.'

If you find that your need for life insurance is still an important part of your contingency plan, but the problem is that the economic downturn has made it too expensive, consider ways to cut your costs and help your cash flow. 'It's a matter of prioritising the premium cost into your household spending budget,' says Chris Rutherford. 'You could pay your premium by the month. Or you can reduce your level of cover. But don't just cancel your policy without thinking it through. If you have an adviser, they can assist you with options.'

Certainty in a recession

In an economic downturn, insurance can give you some security. For example, if illness meant you were unable to work and your mortgage repayments became unaffordable, selling your home could take a lot longer in the downturn, or you may have to settle for a lower price. Adequate income replacement insurance could have avoided that forced sale.

If you're working you probably already have insurance through super – check the level of life, disability and income protection insurance you're already paying for. If you don't have enough cover, consider buying more units. But if you're paying for insurance you don't feel you need, consider cancelling some units so that the money is directed into your superannuation investments instead. It doesn't have to be an 'all or nothing' decision. Carefully consider the benefits you'd lose by cancelling or reducing insurance – it could be a mistake.

**Do
this
today**

On the other hand, if your need for cover has increased, consider increasing your insurance through your superannuation fund – there are few cheaper ways.

19

Ten things not to do

The recession may lead to a desperate search for get-rich-quick solutions, but don't make a bad situation worse.

Here are ten mistakes to avoid in this period of economic downturn.

1 *Fail to diversify*

The people who get themselves into the worst financial difficulties are often those who put their money in just one asset or investment. If you invested all your money in the Australian share index at its high in late 2007, for example, it would have been worth 50% less by early 2009. If you put it all in one badly performing company – such as ABC Learning Centres or Babcock & Brown – you might have lost over 90%. Remember, diversifying your money between different investments and asset classes spreads the risk.

2 *Keep financial problems to yourself*

The earlier you admit to financial difficulties and seek advice, the better. This will often increase the range of options you have. For example, when somebody experiencing mortgage stress informs their lender, this should trigger the lender to implement consumer protection provisions that can help the borrower out of difficulty. The longer the borrower waits the fewer options they'll have.

3 *Make costly switches*

Take your time and consider all the pros and cons before switching from one financial product or institution to another. For example, you might want to switch from your super fund due to poor performance. But will you lose insurance benefits as a result, meaning you'll have to undergo new health tests to get similar cover with another company?

4 *Fail to plan*

Assess your current financial position, your spending and your needs. Consider getting licensed financial advice to help you devise a strategy for the future. Have a plan B.

5 *Under-insure*

Protecting your wealth is just as important as building it. Make sure you consider what insurance you need for your wealth, health, assets and the people who depend on you.

6 *Think you can get high returns at low risk*

Investments don't work that way. With bank deposit interest rates heading south, you might be tempted by investment funds offering twice the interest. But the risks could be much higher than those of a government guaranteed bank deposit - for an extra few per cent interest a debenture may pay (less after income tax) you could risk losing all your capital and interest. It has happened in the past.

7 *Invest in things you don't understand*

The best paid investment bankers in many of the world's biggest and most illustrious financial institutions are wishing they followed that simple piece of advice. It could have prevented the loss of billions of dollars of losses from collateralised debt obligations and other financial innovations. Make sure you fully understand everything you invest in – don't be afraid to ask the most basic questions.

8 *Fall for a scam, trendy product or gimmick*
You've heard it a thousand times before – if it sounds too good to be true, it's not true. So why do so many people continue to fall for scams every year? Don't believe the snake oil salesmen who say getting rich can be quick and easy – it takes time, careful planning and a reasoned approach.

9 *Make quick decisions under pressure*
People often make bad, uninformed decisions when put under duress. This could be due to pressure from sales people, agents and advisers. The best advice is to take your time. When it comes to investing, borrowing and even shopping, the economic downturn means it's a buyer's market.

10 *Under-estimate risks*
Risky strategies are sometimes promoted as a way to solve financial problems – for example, margin loans and options trading. They may work, but make sure you understand the risks and worst case scenario. Some people who used the equity in their property to borrow to invest in shares, for example, experienced big losses and financial difficulties when markets crashed.

Finally, there are lots of great resources available that you can draw on in your recession-busting quest. The Appendix to this book suggests websites and publications that can help you cut costs on your everyday expenses, make better decisions with your money and arm yourself with even more knowledge to survive the downturn. The world economy is on shaky ground and we could be in for a rocky ride – but there's plenty we can all do to take control of our personal economies.

Appendix

Useful contacts and resources

Here is a list of some of the resources that may help you in your quest to become recession-proof.

CHOICE

For independent research and testing that will help you save money and buy better products and services, go to <www.choice.com.au>.

Investments

The Australian Securities Exchange runs education seminars and publishes investor information on its website. A good research resource: <www.asx.com.au>.

Morningstar publishes share and managed fund data, ratings, tools, and analyst commentary to help you manage your portfolio. <www.morningstar.com.au>.

The Investment and Financial Services Association <www.ifsa.com. au> is an industry group representing the main fund managers, retail super funds, and life insurance companies. It publishes consumer fact sheets around investment and insurance.

The Eureka Report, an online financial newsletter, provide analysis and opinion: <www.eurekareport.com.au>.

Banking and borrowing

Canstar Cannex <www.canstar.com.au> and RateCity <www.rate city.com.au> are comparison sites for a wide range of financial services products. Infochoice compares a range of banking, borrowing and investment products <www.infochoice.com.au>.

Your entitlements

Contact Centrelink for advice about payments and benefits you could be entitled to, as well as free resources and the Newstart Allowance that could help you get back on your feet. Go to <www.centrelink. gov.au>. To make an appointment with a Centrelink Financial Information Service (FIS) Officer call 13 23 00.

The Australian Taxation Office can provide information about the often complex regulations surrounding super, information about income and capital gains tax, severance packages, Employment Termination Payments, tax-free thresholds and lots more. <www. ato.gov.au/individuals>.

Superannuation

The Association of Superannuation Funds of Australia's website has fact sheets and consumer guides, and publishes the Westpac-ASFA Retirement Standard index: <www.asfa.asn.au>.

Investment and Financial Services Association: <www.ifsa.com.au>
Australian Institute of Superannuation Trustees:< www.aist.asn.au>.

The following websites provide information comparing super fund performance:

Chant West <www.chantwest.com.au>
SelectingSuper <www.selectingsuper.com.au>
SuperRatings <www.superratings.com.au>
Australian Prudential Regulation Authority <www.apra.gov.au>.

Financial regulators

Check the company you're dealing with is licensed at the Australian Securities and Investments Commission's website <www.asic.gov.au>. ASIC's consumer site – <www.fido.gov.au> – has information about most financial products and services. Its calculators can help you work out the cost of borrowing, calculate the effect of fees on investment performance, and estimate what your super will be worth when you retire. The Australian Prudential Regulation Authority is charged with ensuring the safety and viability of our banking, insurance and superannuation systems. It also regulates the trustees of super funds and registers the funds and lists the Authorised Deposit Taking Institutions – banks, building societies and credit unions – to which the government deposit guarantee applies. Go to <www.apra.gov.au>.

Complaints schemes

The Credit Ombudsman Service deals with complaints about lenders and brokers. Phone 1800 138 422, 02 9273 8400 or visit <www.cosl.com.au>.

The Financial Ombudsman Service is an approved external dispute resolution scheme for member financial services providers. If you have a complaint you can't resolve, call 1300 780 808 or visit <www.fos.org.au>.

Career

If you're interested in upgrading your skills and training, check out the Seek Learning website for ideas <www.seeklearning.com.au>. It provides links to education and training resources.

Stress and anxiety about money

The recession can lead to difficult times for people, especially those who have lost a job, seen their investments or wealth plummet, or are suffering from mortgage stress. beyondblue may be able to help: go to <www.beyondblue.org.au> or call 1300 224 636.

For details of a free financial counselling service near you, check the phone book or search for financial counsellors at <www.asic.gov.au>.

Retirement investments

Strategies for investing your money after you retire are outside the scope of this book. For information about your various pension and income stream options, contact the National Information Centre on Retirement Investments <www.nicri.org.au>. The author of this book represents CHOICE on NICRI's Advisory Committee.

Shopping and saving

Get money saving tips from websites like <www. simplesavings.com.au> and <www.cheapskates.com.au>

Property

House price data is available from <www.rpdata.com.au>, <www.residex.com.au> and <www.homepriceguide.com.au>.
For tips and warnings for property buyers and sellers, check out <www.jenman.com.au>.

Index